3 STORY™: THE SECRET HISTORY OF THE GIANT MAN

Matt

3 STORY™

THE SECRET HISTORY OF THE GIANT MAN

Written and illustrated by MATT KINDT

President and Publisher **MIKE RICHARDSON**

Expanded Edition Editor **DANIEL CHABON**

Expanded Edition Assistant Editor **BRETT ISRAEL**

First Edition Editor **DIANA SCHUTZ**

First Edition Assistant Editor **BRENDAN WRIGHT**

Designer **ETHAN KIMBERLING**

Digital Art Technician **ALLYSON HALLER**

Published by Dark Horse Books
A division of Dark Horse Comics, Inc.
10956 SE Main Street
Milwaukie, OR 97222

DarkHorse.com

To find a comics shop in your area,
visit comicshoplocator.com

First edition: August 2018
ISBN 978-1-50670-622-1
Digital ISBN 978-1-50670-623-8

10 9 8 7 6 5 4 3 2 1
Printed in China

3 Story: The Secret History of the Giant Man

Library of Congress Cataloging-in-Publication Data

Names: Kindt, Matt, writer, illustrator.
Title: 3 story : the secret history of the giant man / written and illustrated by Matt Kindt.
Other titles: Three story | Secret history of the giant man
Description: Expanded edition. | First edition. | Milwaukie, OR : Dark Horse Books, August 2018.
Identifiers: LCCN 2018006926 | ISBN 9781506706221 (paperback)
Subjects: LCSH: Graphic novels. | BISAC: COMICS & GRAPHIC NOVELS / Fantasy. | COMICS & GRAPHIC NOVELS / General.
Classification: LCC PN6727.K54 A16 2018 | DDC 741.5/973--dc23
LC record available at https://lccn.loc.gov/2018006926

1ST STORY

Is that the radio...?
Louis Armstrong...

Oh, Butchy...
What happened?
Butch, you loved Louis...
Too rough for me...

I tolerated it though...
For you...

Funny how I can't remember your face...
Your voice...

I remember the vague outline...
The soft rhythm of your voice...

Not the words.
Just the sound.

No detail.

Just a sketch...

Why is the only part I want to remember...
...so short, Butchy?

And everything...

I want...

To
forget...

Is...

So...

Long.

The best moments so short.

So much easier to forget.
You...
Me...
Even Craig...

End up disappearing.

And the roses. You didn't know me long enough to know I never really liked roses.
But there they were.

The very idea of you managing to have them delivered from wherever you were in France...

CHEVAL NOIR
Like a magic trick.

*

He came up to me after he found out those flowers was sent.

He says, "What the hell was you thinking, Billy?!"

And I told him I was looking out for his green ass...

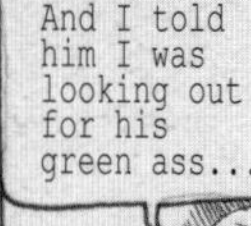

And he says, "Billy, I know you was trying to do good..."

"But you need to pull yer head out! I done saved yer life twice, and damned if I'll do it again!"

I didn't know what to say. And then he says...

"Marge don't like roses! She hates 'em! The only flower she don't like!"

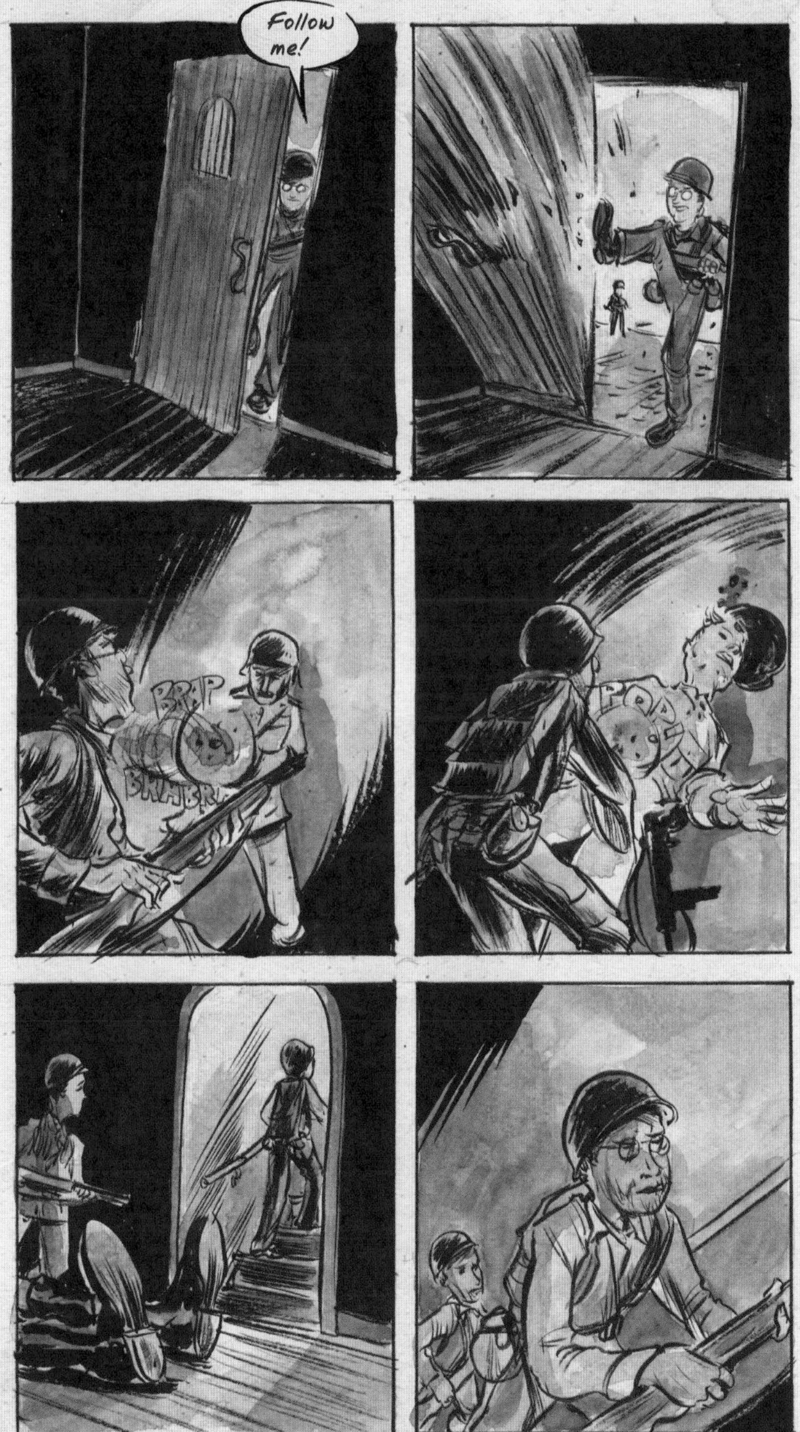
Follow me!
BRAP

Do you see the sniper?

I coulda swore he was up here.
Get down!

POP
There!

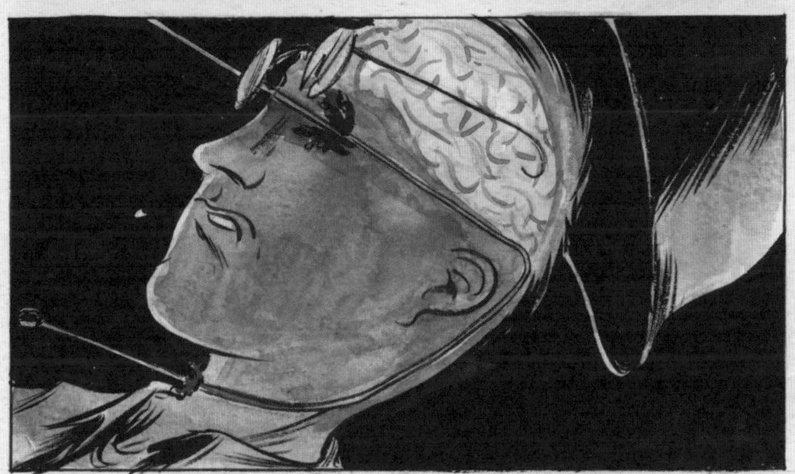

Like a magic trick.

You disappearing...

And flowers in your place...

But then the show ended. And the magician disappeared.

But I was left on stage -- still expected to perform.

WAAH!
And I just wanted...

I just wanted the curtain to drop on everythins.
WAAH WAAH

And, Butchy? The bisser our baby sot...

ACON
MALTESE
BOGART
FALCON
The less of you there was...

And this baby overshadowed everythins.

Ma! Ma!
I can dress myself!
Okay, okay. You don't have to yell.

Like a magic trick.

The scarf is supposed to disappear.

But something goes wrong.
It doesn't disappear.

It's still painfully, awkwardly there.

JUNE 1955
I think we should call the doctor.
The worst part was that any hope I had of Craig replacing you, Butchy..?

Disappeared
when he was eight.

Well...we might be able to try a few things...

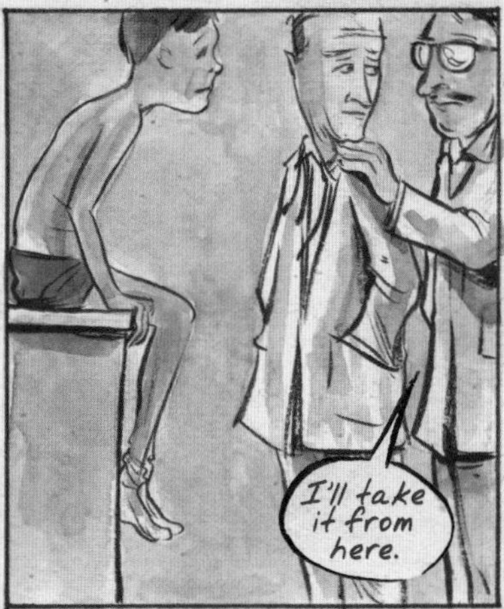
I'll take it from here.

And the bigger he got, the less I could hold on to him...or you.
More, please!

9 years old.
Well, I'm stumped.

10 years old.
We need to run more tests.

11 years old.
Frankly, we don't know what to do.

Are you feeling okay?
Yes.

12 years old.
Doctor, a word...

I think we should maybe take steps to follow the directives I laid out earlier...

There wasn't any stopping him, Butchy.
06

Just like there was no holding onto you...

All I could do...

Was watch
it happen.

Giant Boy in Town!

Local boy Craig Pressgang has been making a sensation of late. He is currently the tallest 8-year-old in recorded history and is on pace to break Robert Wadlow's record-setting height of nearly 9 feet. When asked how he felt about being taller than all of his fellow classmates, young Craig replied, "No different really. I like cowboys and robots, just like the next fella."

Giant Boy Grows Up

Hometown celebrity Craig Pressgang is making headlines again. Since last we checked in with young Craig (age 10), he has grown a whopping twelve inches! We asked Craig's mother, Marge, how she's dealing with her son's incredible growth. "Well, I hope he doesn't outgrow the house. He's a good boy, though. Very mindful and loves to help around the house. He's a dream to have around when it's time to trim the trees."

Too Tall for Basketball

Craig "3 Story" Pressgang is making headlines again. But this time he's causing a little trouble. Neighboring towns are protesting the eligibility of Craig for the local basketball team, our own Buffalo Bills. Teams claim Craig's freakish growth spurts are giving him an unfair advantage against opponents, and they might have a point. The Bills have been trampling opponents in every game this season starting with their crosstown *(cont.)*

Giant Sighting

Craig Pressgang sightings have become akin to Bigfoot. Craig's mother informed the *Times* that he rarely leaves the house, but one eyewitness recently claimed she saw Craig's towering frame vacationing on the lake front in nearby Cheektowaga, New York. "He was lumbering around. It almost seemed like he was moving in slow motion. And I think I saw him with a girl. Maybe his mother?" Other sources are saying that *(cont.)*

He grew up and away, Butchy.

And it was like that Cary Grant movie we saw...
Where he's a good guy, maybe...or he could be a murderer.

You're left wondering which way it's going to go.

And I liked to
think it was going to
go my way.

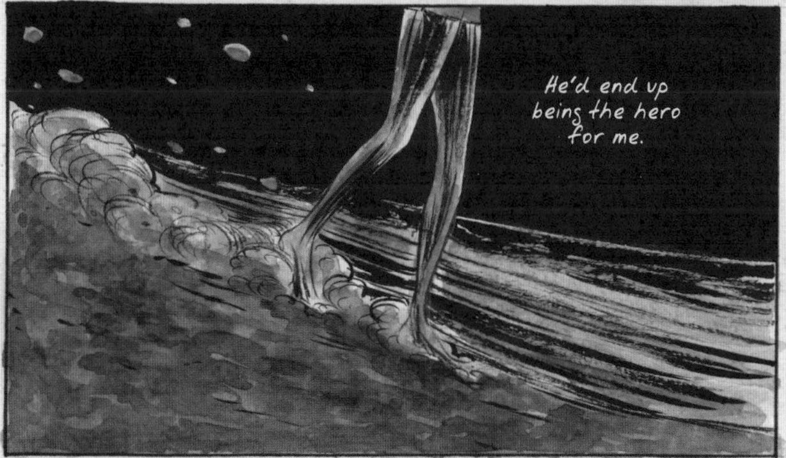
He'd end up
being the hero
for me.

But I realized
that, either
way...I wasn't
Joan Fontaine
to Cary Grant.

I was the hat-check girl they walk by on the way to the rest of their lives.

It didn't mean anything.

It ended up being like an early chapter in a long novel.

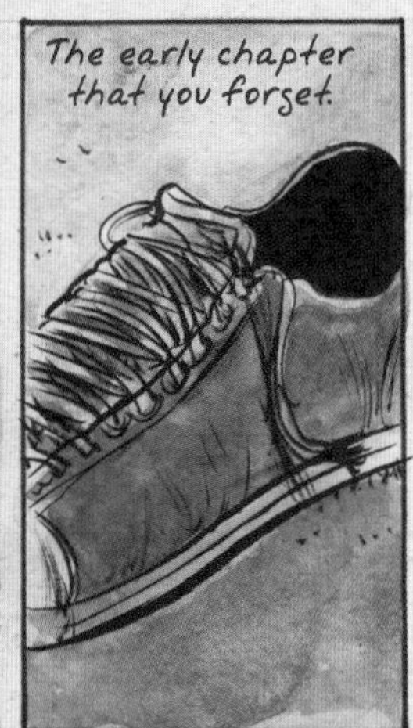
The early chapter that you forget.

I think I ended up knowing him as well as you did, Butchy.

Help!

Ouch!

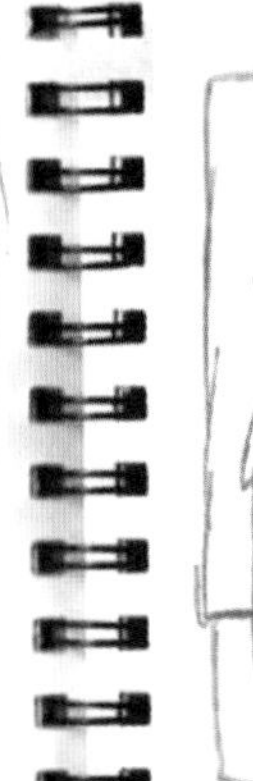

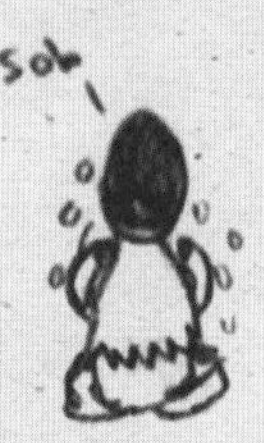
sob

YARD
SALE
TODAY
210 OAKWOOD

How much for these shoes?

Giant Education

Hometown icon and hero Craig Pressgang attended his first days of college at Elmhurst College in the suburbs of Chicago.

Craig's height of 9 feet caused distractions early on, but, from eyewitness reports, the student body quickly welcomed its newest and most famous student. Several colleges vied for Craig's enrollment, but Elmhurst finally won out.

Craig plans to study economics and business, but his major is still undecided. The campus has already taken steps to accommodate its largest student by modifying an existing dorm room to house Craig comfortably.

"I couldn't ask for a better roommate," Ray Cool said when questioned about rooming with the "Giant Man." "He's quiet and keeps to himself mostly. He's just a student like anyone else here on

NDA
Oddly, I stopped caring, Butchy. The distance between us made it easy.

Clothing the Giant

Craig Pressgang, our own giant man, recently signed a lucrative deal with Haggar clothier. In addition to his signing bonus, the large clothing manufacturer will provide Craig with custom outfits, including large-scale slacks, shirts, jackets, and even ties.

When asked what prompted the deal, executives at

He had his life. I had mine again.
That's what I tell myself.

I decided to take care of Mother. I think you only met her the once.

rings
rings

Is Craig there?

It's Marge. His mother.

I'm sure he's busy. Too busy to talk, I guess.

He missed his grandmother's birthday. I just wanted to...

It's too far for me. He can't afford to take a week away?

I see.

click

I know exactly why I saw Mother.
A sad last attempt.

To be something for her.
What I'd wanted you and Craig to be for me.

The gray light in her eyes told me I was too late.
But at least I tried.

Like a magic trick...

Where you disappeared...

And then at the end...

...returned
triumphant
in a cloud of
smoke.

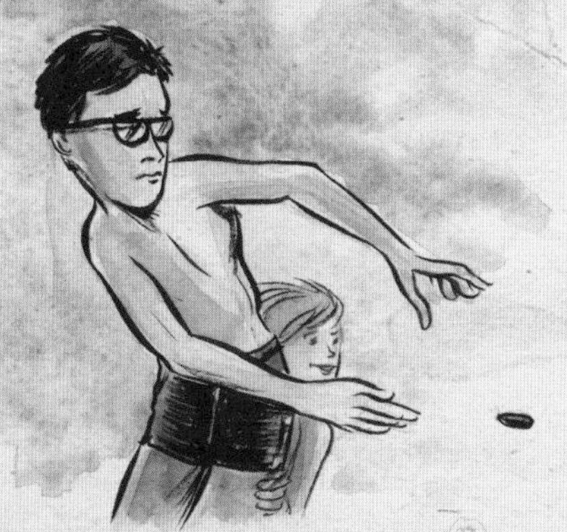
But he was too big...

Like the elephant in the room...
The only way to make something like that disappear...

Is to stop talking about it.

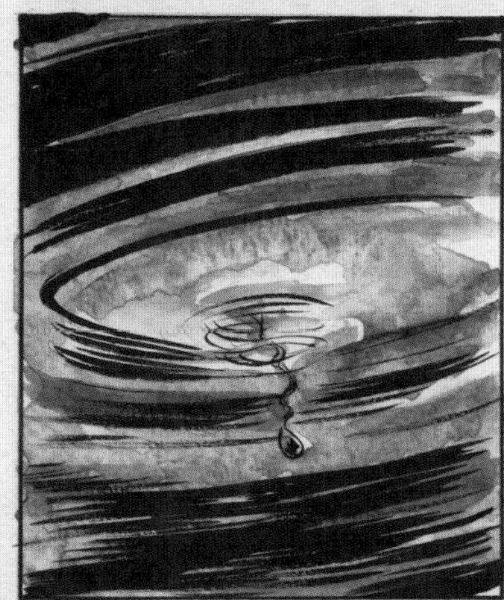

You knew Cary Grant would turn out to be innocent.

He was too big a star.

Too big to
disappoint.

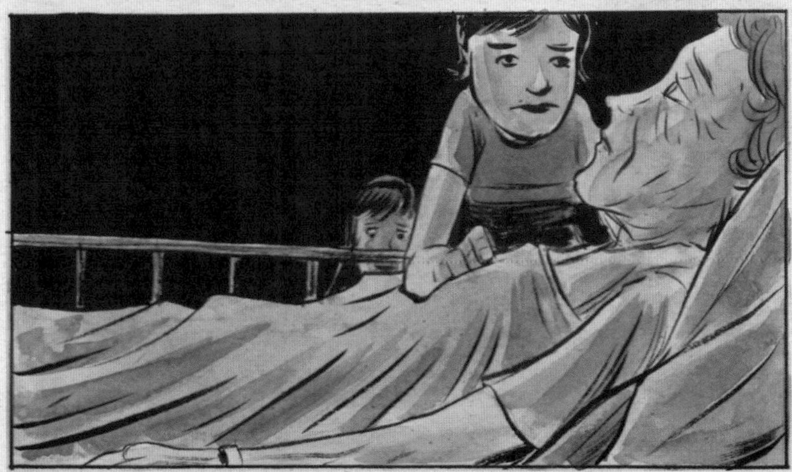

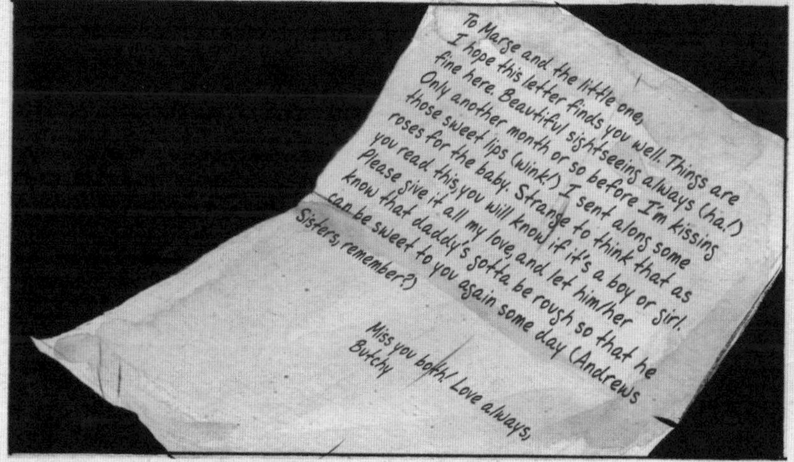

To Marge and the little one,
I hope this letter finds you well. Things are
fine here. Beautiful sightseeing always (ha!)
Only another month or so before I'm kissing
those sweet lips (wink!) I sent along some
roses for the baby. Strange to think that as
you read this, you will know if it's a boy or girl.
Please give it all my love, and let him/her
know that daddy's gotta be rough so that he
can be sweet to you again some day (Andrews
Sisters, remember?)

Miss you both! Love always,
Butchy

2ND STORY

I was in love
that summer.

In love with
the summer.
With the air.

And the
freedom
from home...

I was in
love with
ideas...

I like your
hands...

I'd always been interested in how things fit together.

I'd find an
outlet later.

In architecture.

ting
ting
And sounds.
Quiet.
And lonely.
ting
ting

ting
ting
ting

ting

ting

I saw Craig Presssans that summer, too.

But I wouldn't realize it until later that fall.

Oh, man!
I think that was my bus!

Can I get ahead...?
Wait yer turn like every-body else.

If you walk out that door, don't bother to come back! You hear me?!

Come back

The next bus isn't until...

...tomorrow...
That Fall at school I saw him again.
And I got that sinking feeling of disaster and happiness all at once.

That weird chemical reaction that I try to make my brain generate with every guy...it rarely works.

He's my roommate, y'know.
Who?
That tall guy?

The Giant Man!
Yeah, where've you been?

I've been taking notes for him...

He just can't fit in the lecture halls anymore.
He's going to the protest rally in exchange for my notes.
You're using him..?

Just hold this up and look angry.

Big Man at Protest

The anti-war rally held on campus yesterday evening was the best attended yet, say local organizers. Some of this may be attributable to the protestors' latest recruit, Craig Pressgang, the giant man hailing from Buffalo, New York. When questioned about his participation, Craig politely shrugged and claimed to be helping out a friend.

Front page, eh?!
Ha! He looks miserable.

What's he like?
I don't know. He's quiet, y'know?

I think a lot of people are just intimidated by him. Makes him hard to approach.
?

In the late 1960s, young Craig became a straight-A student and often participated in friendly rallies to promote local events and causes.

He lent his unique talents and affable personality to many great causes and helped everyone he knew. Those closest to him agreed: he was outgoing, personable, and "just another one of the guys."

Craig would go on to graduate with honors. He received a degree in business, and he even found time to take some art classes. He especially enjoyed creating art, having the most fun and success with his famous "hand prints."

Imagine giving everyone you meet short-man syndrome.

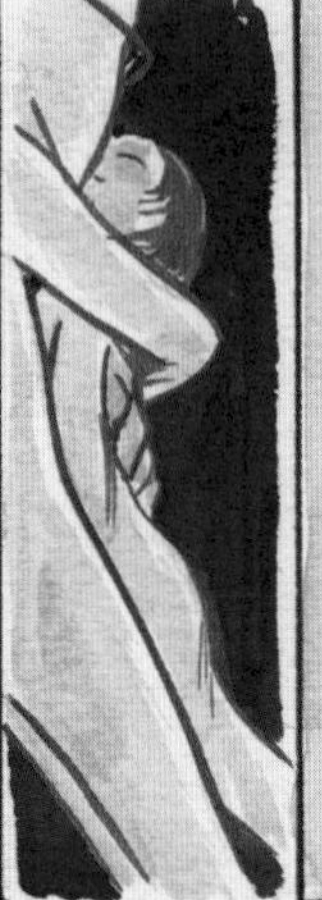

Oh, yeah. Almost forgot.

In case you get bored this weekend, we're having an...event.

TURTLE RACE
FRIDAY NIGHT
It was as exciting as it sounded.

yawn
But I got to talk to Craig.

* Elapsed time: 2 seconds

I didn't want you to come if you didn't want to.
It was a scam all along!

Gino's would end up being one of my first miniatures.
I hadn't realized that at the time. All I noticed was how much Craig could eat.

A lot.
All subsidized by the school. He brought press and increased enrollment.

He was big by then. Big enough that we couldn't go anywhere without being noticed.
I didn't mind it.
In fact, I liked it. The attention reflecting off him and onto me.

But it wasn't all selfish. I really loved him.
And I felt like he appreciated having someone to go to. To reflect some of the focus onto.

It was strange at first. Like loving a hurricane or an earthquake.

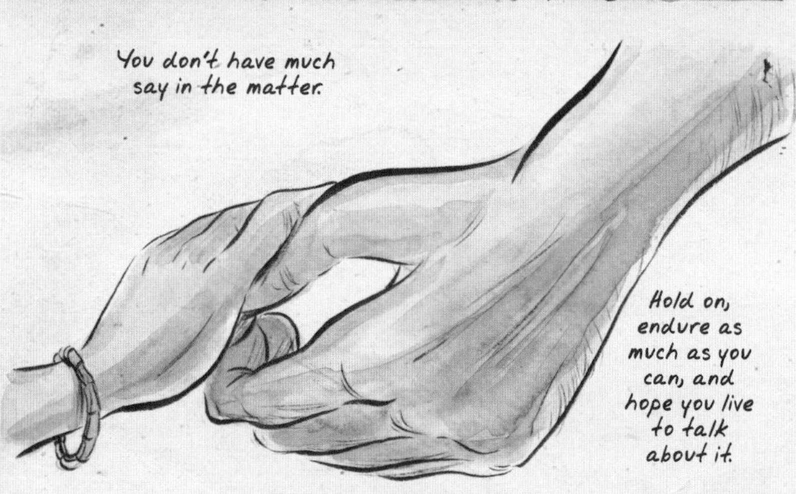
You don't have much say in the matter.
Hold on, endure as much as you can, and hope you live to talk about it.

I heard the whispers, of course, and jokes about his size.
But he was perfect then. It would be the only time in our lives that we were truly compatible.

One winter.

A small window of opportunity.

I didn't know you were painting.
Yeah.
I need something when I get too big to read the textbooks.

You don't need textbooks. These are beautiful.

Galleries like 'em. But all they want are the big hand prints.

He told me once that shared experience was the one thing that made him forget his size.

Talking about a baseball game. Or politics...

...reporting live from Dallas...

...the President has been shot...

ITHSONIAN
I never thought about how out of place he was until I saw his things out of context.

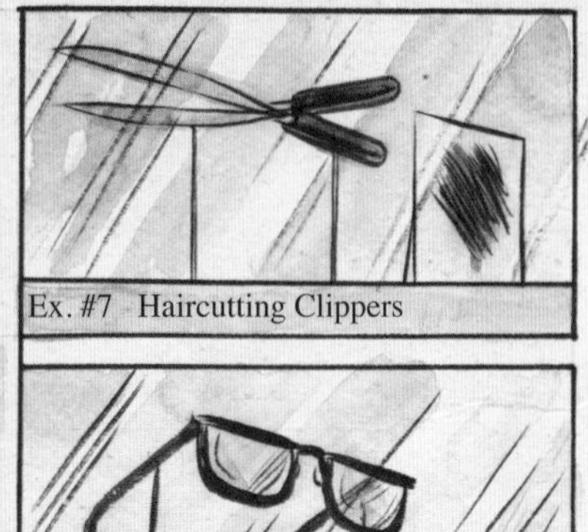
Ex. #7 Haircutting Clippers
Ex. #22 Glasses

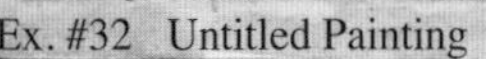
Ex. #32 Untitled Painting

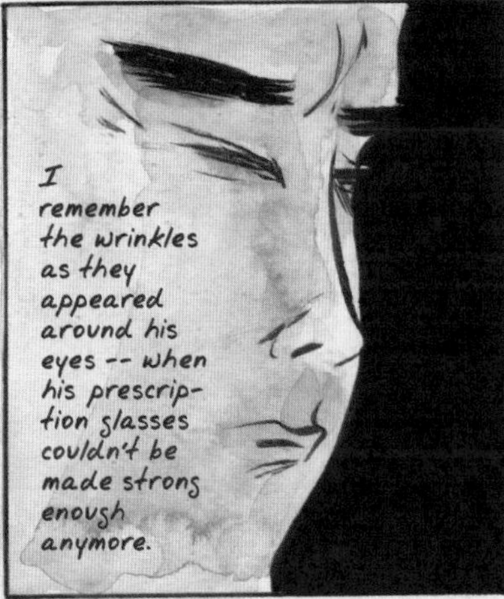
I remember the wrinkles as they appeared around his eyes -- when his prescrip-tion glasses couldn't be made strong enough anymore.

And the phone that I hated.
Ex. #27 Phone

RING RING
It shocked me every time I picked it up. A short in the wires.
RING RING

I can't hear anything. Can you talk?

Holding that phone was like a Pavlovian experiment.
Hello, Mrs. Pressgang ...Mom?
I'm not your mother.

Ask her to come out.
We'd like to have you visit. Before the wedding.

Stop playing games. Put him on the phone.
Tell her we'll buy the ticket.

No? Well I hope you're happy.

You're busy?
Busy taking care of MY mother.
CLIK

Okay then. Maybe after Christmas?

Ah!

Stupid!

GIANT takes you away from the everyday

3ut you don't smoke," she says.
e replies: "I know, I know. It's more of a trade, really. I endorse them, and
ey hire someone to manufacture my clothes. I get to keep the suit from the
ioto shoot." She didn't like it but went along with it anyway. He wasn't
ping to stop growing. That much was clear. So every hour, every day he
ent doing something else, was time she–they–would never get back.
He interrupted her thought and continued talking in his low baritone. "I wonder if they
ould make me a giant cigarette. That'd be kind of funny. They'd probably call the fire department on me."
She gave him a wan smile. Well, at least she'd finally get to see Paris.

Craig was too big for the dorm our senior year. My final project ended up being the design of a house for him.

Finally, a place that would fit him. He could fit in.

Local Chicago businesses funded everything, and my first architectural job was going to be his home.

Our home.

Something really tall!
I would never see him happier.
Lots of windows!

Big doorways!
And on the roof -- one of those walk-ways...?
Widow's walk?
Yeah! But shaped like a ship deck!

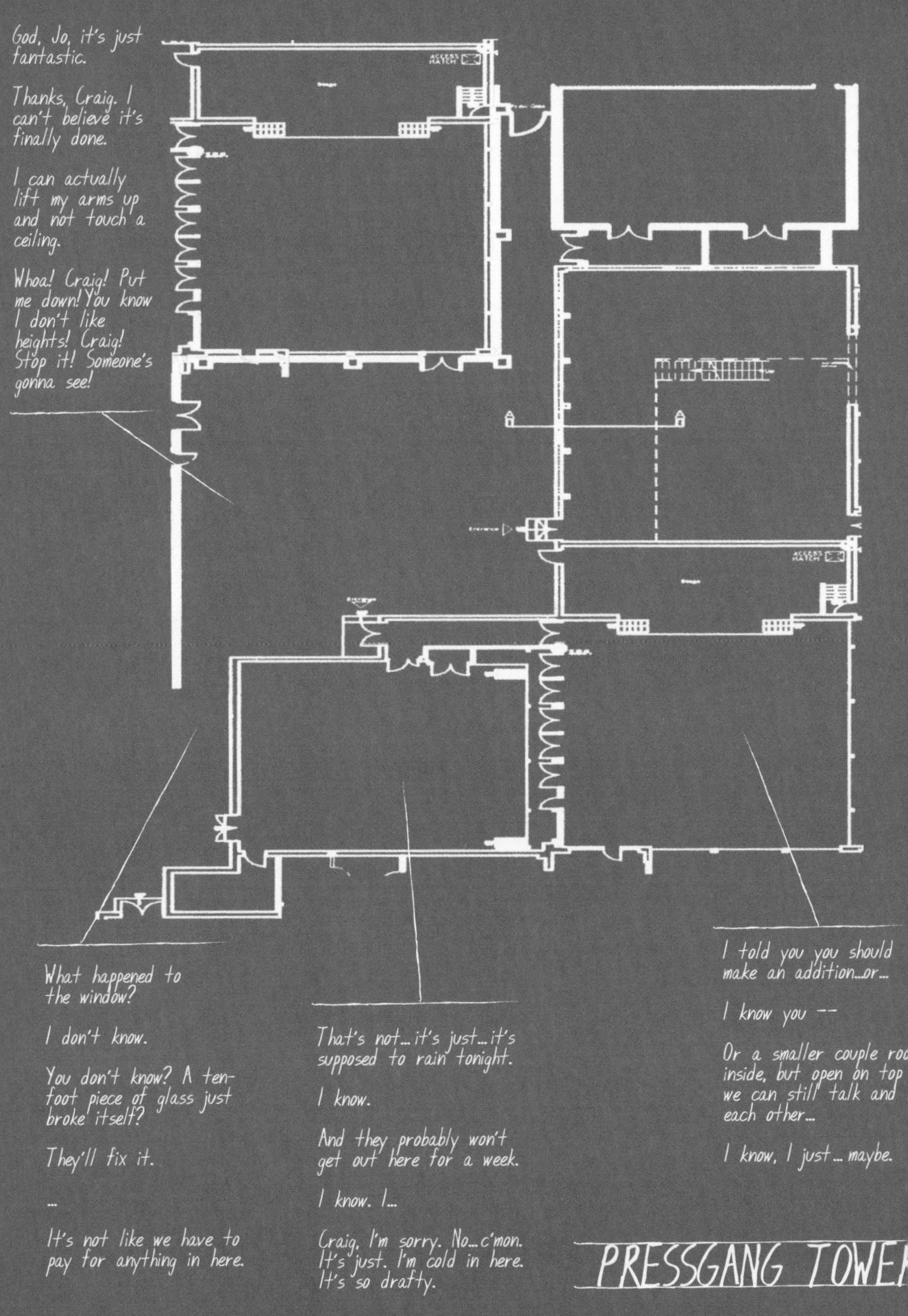
God, Jo, it's just fantastic.
Thanks, Craig. I can't believe it's finally done.
I can actually lift my arms up and not touch a ceiling.
Whoa! Craig! Put me down! You know I don't like heights! Craig! Stop it! Someone's gonna see!
What happened to the window?
I don't know.
You don't know? A ten-foot piece of glass just broke itself?
They'll fix it.
...
It's not like we have to pay for anything in here.
That's not... it's just... it's supposed to rain tonight.
I know.
And they probably won't get out here for a week.
I know. I...
Craig, I'm sorry. No... c'mon. It's just. I'm cold in here. It's so drafty.
I told you you should make an addition... or...
I know you --
Or a smaller couple ro
inside, but open on top
we can still talk and
each other...
I know, I just... maybe.
PRESSGANG TOWE

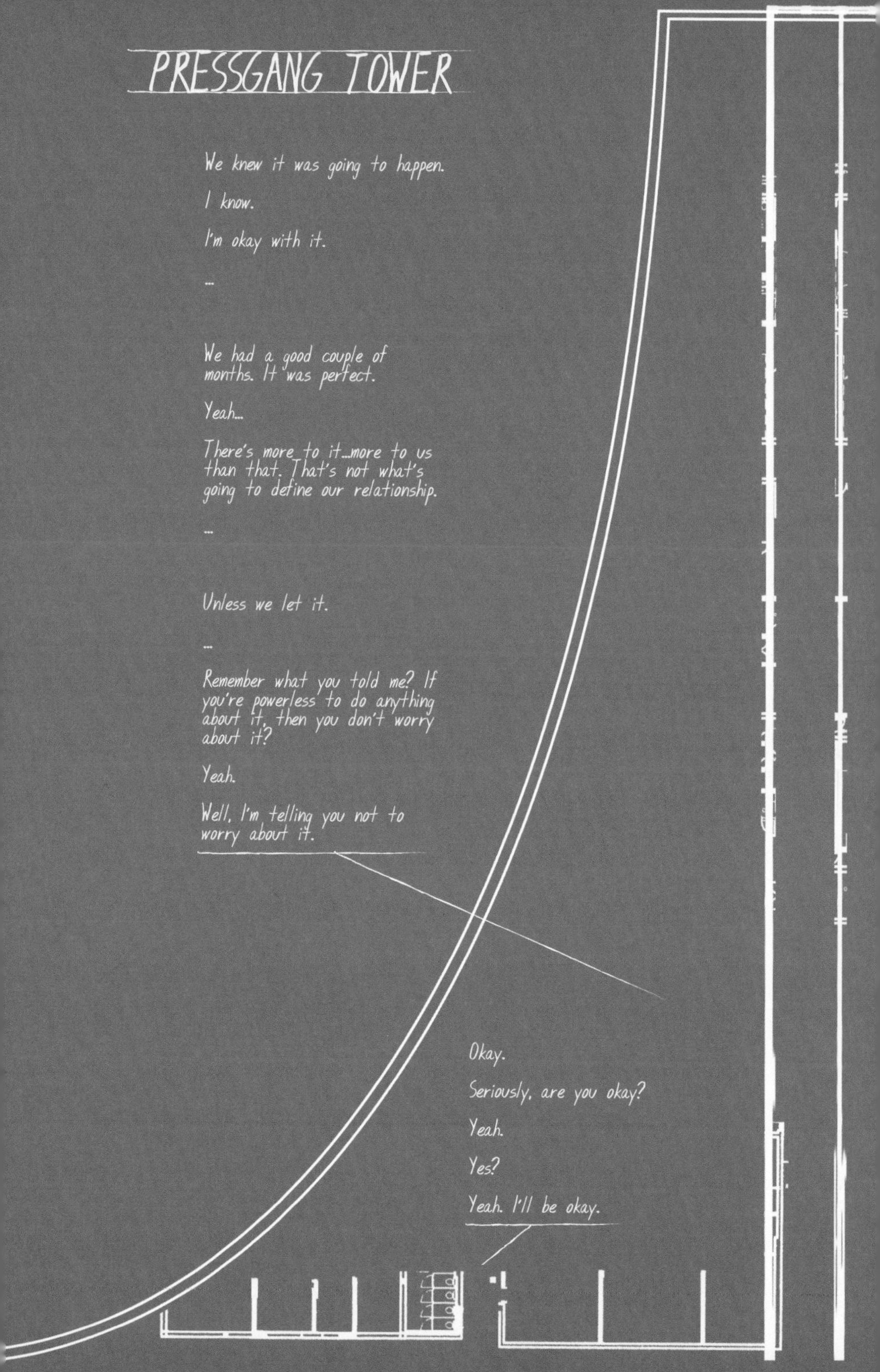

PRESSGANG TOWER

We knew it was going to happen.

I know.

I'm okay with it.

...

We had a good couple of months. It was perfect.

Yeah...

There's more to it...more to us than that. That's not what's going to define our relationship.

...

Unless we let it.

...

Remember what you told me? If you're powerless to do anything about it, then you don't worry about it?

Yeah.

Well, I'm telling you not to worry about it.

Okay.

Seriously, are you okay?

Yeah.

Yes?

Yeah. I'll be okay.

He got bigger and
bigger, of course.

And I'd be
lying...

If I said
I wasn't
scared...

Scared of his proposal.
Scared of what he would become.
Scared of being with him.
Scared of our future.

But
we
did
it.

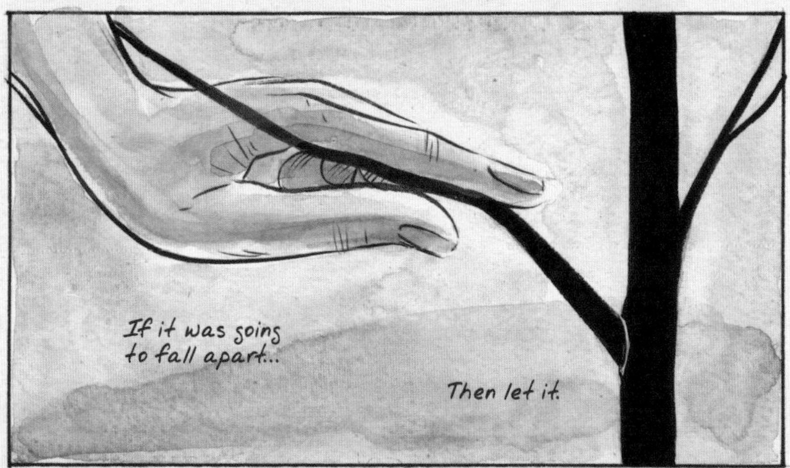
If it was going
to fall apart...
Then let it.

Who else did
he have?

Who was going to
look out for him?

started out as small as any child. But as he grew, so did his art. Some of his larger pieces stand at three stories tall and use over 1,000 gallons of paint.

The sheer size of Craig's larger still-lifes and outdoor scenes makes them not only cost-prohibitive to the average art enthusiast, but also exhibition-prohibitive. Most of Craig's larger works are being stored in government facilities and by the Smithsonian Institute in Washington, D.C.

This is not to say that Craig's art does not sell. The demand for his signature hand-print canvases is still high. The size of these pieces varies depending on the year they were created, with his earlier hand prints, measuring a comparatively modest four feet wide, fetching the highest prices among collectors. When asked about this phenomenon, the

(continued on following page)

A family gathers at one of Craig's outdoor exhibits.

You don't remember me, do you?

Should I?
I watched you grow up.
Yeah, yeah. I remember you.

You were the second doctor, who always came in late to my appointments.

You weren't a doctor, were you?

Well, technically, yes. I was assigned to you. *

We know about the abdominal pains you've been having.

We're worried it's your appendix.
We can take care of it.
And you.

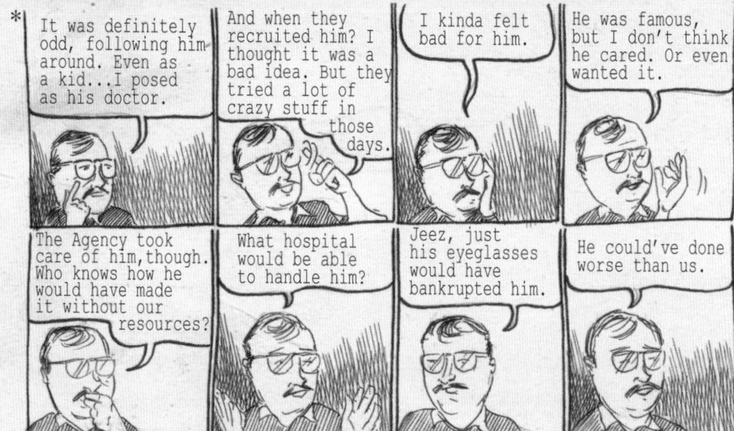
*
It was definitely odd, following him around. Even as a kid...I posed as his doctor.
And when they recruited him? I thought it was a bad idea. But they tried a lot of crazy stuff in those days.
I kinda felt bad for him.
He was famous, but I don't think he cared. Or even wanted it.
The Agency took care of him, though. Who knows how he would have made it without our resources?
What hospital would be able to handle him?
Jeez, just his eyeglasses would have bankrupted him.
He could've done worse than us.

--and your wife and family. You wouldn't have to worry about anything anymore.

We can clothe you. Provide medical aid. Prescription glasses. We're prepared to offer you lifetime benefits.

What company are you with?

CIA.

We need to do a few tests.
What's new.

We have new technology. We might be able to find a way to help you.

Any history of disease in your family?

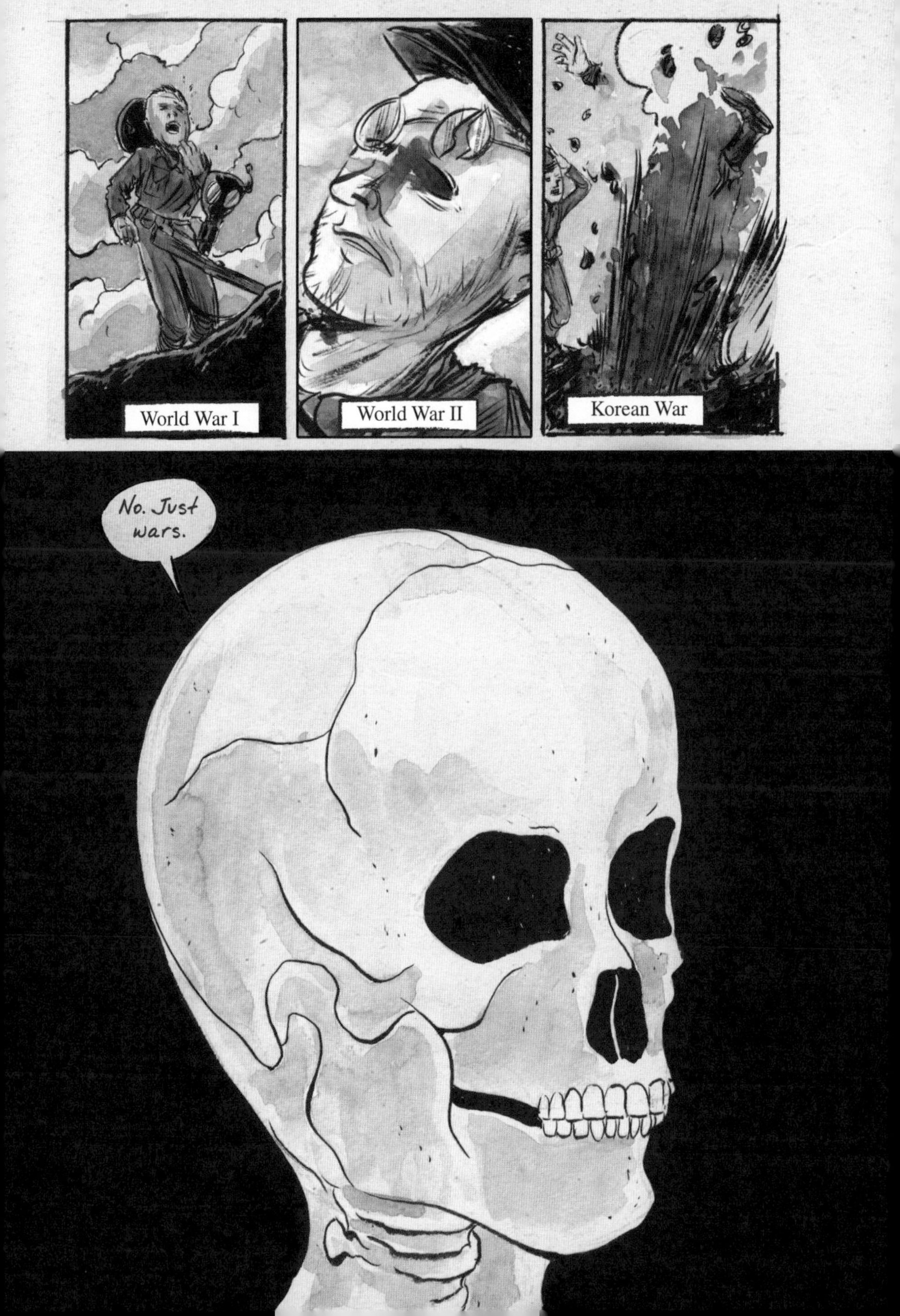

No. Just wars.

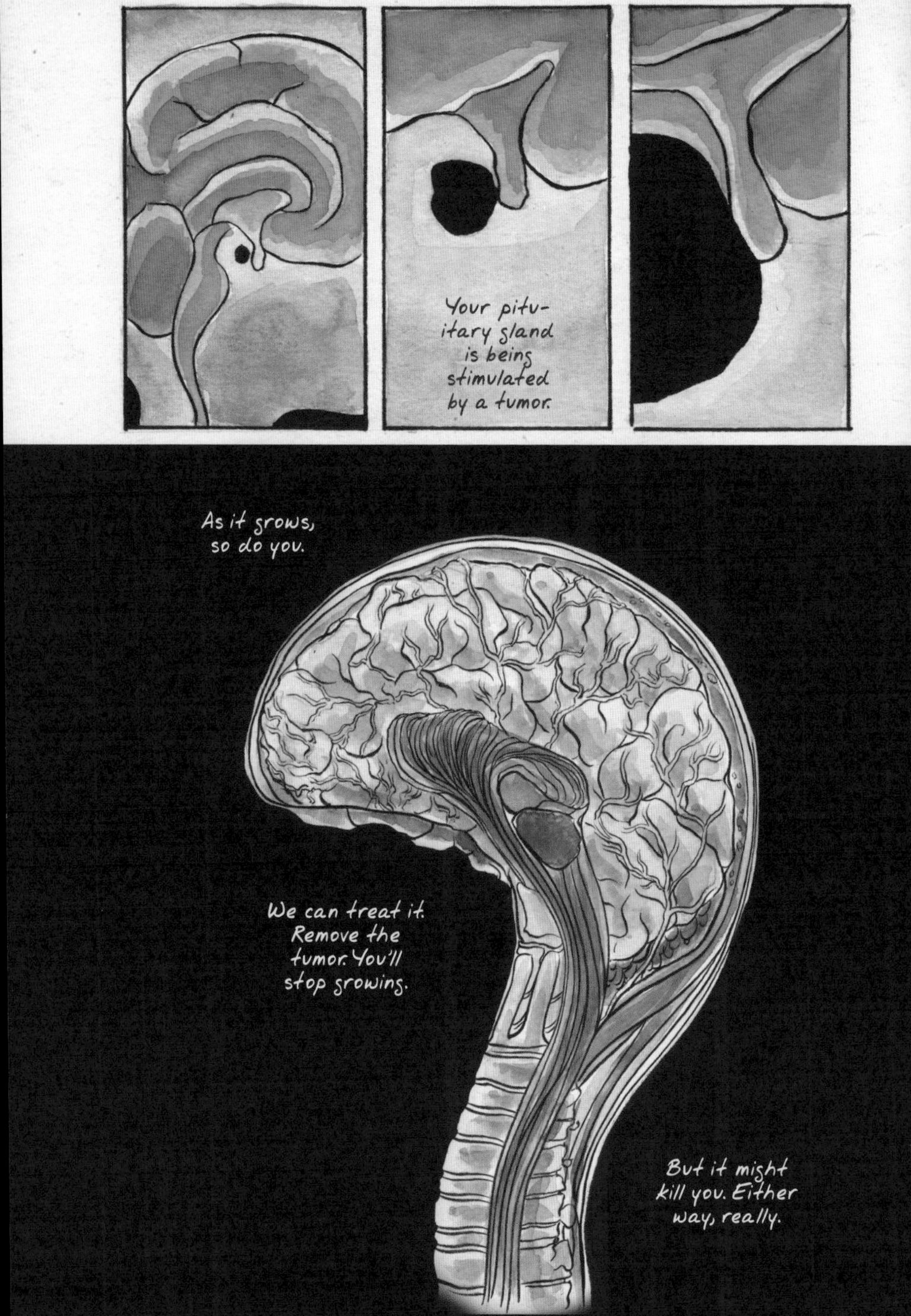

Your pitu-
itary gland
is being
stimulated
by a tumor.

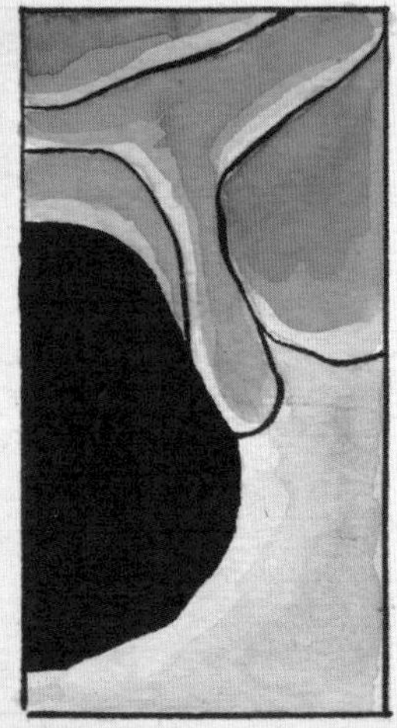

As it grows,
so do you.

We can treat it.
Remove the
tumor. You'll
stop growing.

But it might
kill you. Either
way, really.

Leave it be.

Then let's talk about your nerves.
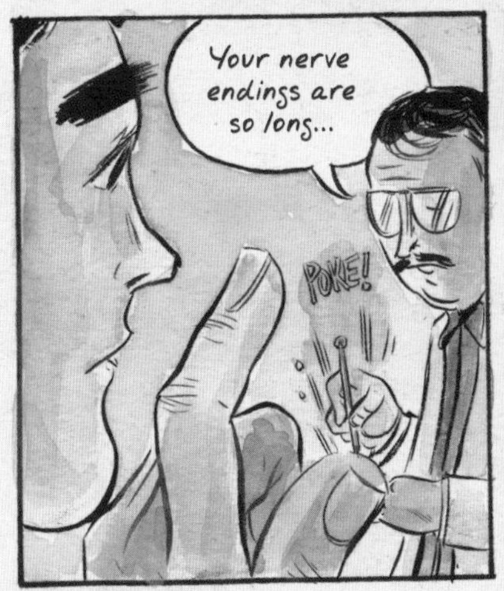
Your nerve endings are so long...
POKE!

You'll need to be careful...

There's a delay.

OW!

You've heard of Robert Wadlow?

The "Giant of Illinois"? Yeah. My mother told me about him when I was younger...

Robert Wadlow was the tallest Cub Scout—on a boating trip, they wouldn't let him in the boat.

"If you fell in, we wouldn't be able to get you back in the boat," the Cub Scout leader warned.

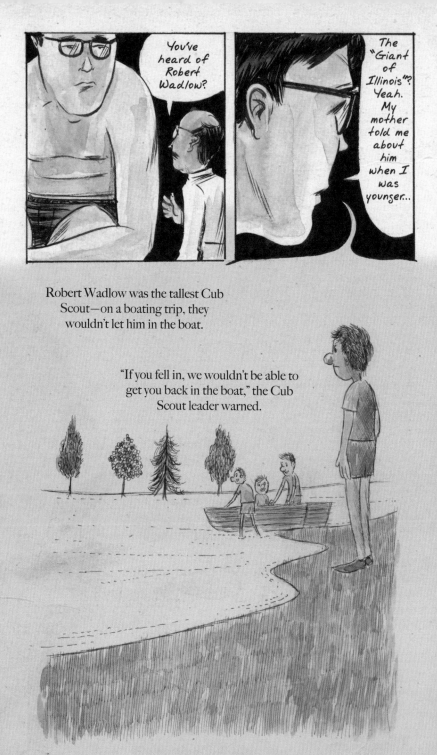

The other boys laughed and enjoyed the boat ride.

They didn't notice that Robert had disappeared.

Slowly, Robert crept up behind the boat, careful not to make a noise.

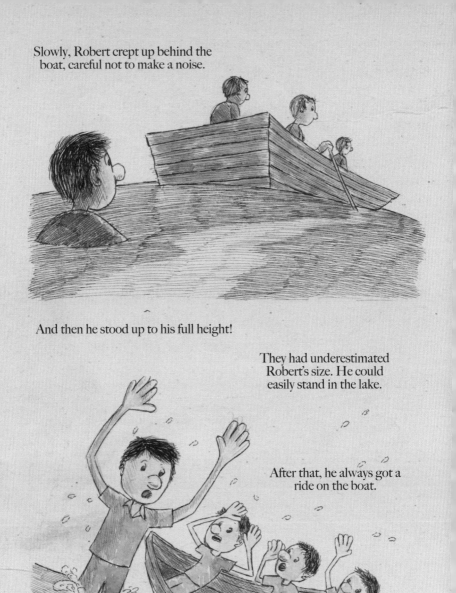

And then he stood up to his full height!

They had underestimated Robert's size. He could easily stand in the lake.

After that, he always got a ride on the boat.

Did she tell you how he died?

No.

Faulty leg braces.
He had to wear specially made leg braces to support himself.
One of the braces cut him on the ankle, and he didn't feel it.

Five days later he died of an infection.

Take care of yourself.

We'll keep you fitted with glasses, but keep taking endorse-ments.

This suit should grow with you to approxi-mately three stories tall. After that, we'll hopefully have engineered a new one.

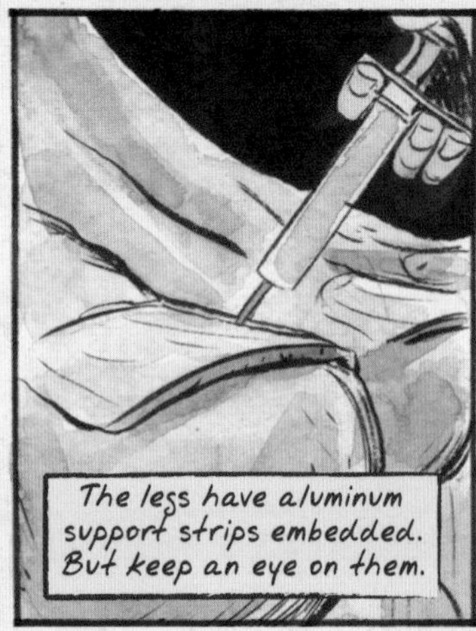
The legs have aluminum support strips embedded. But keep an eye on them.

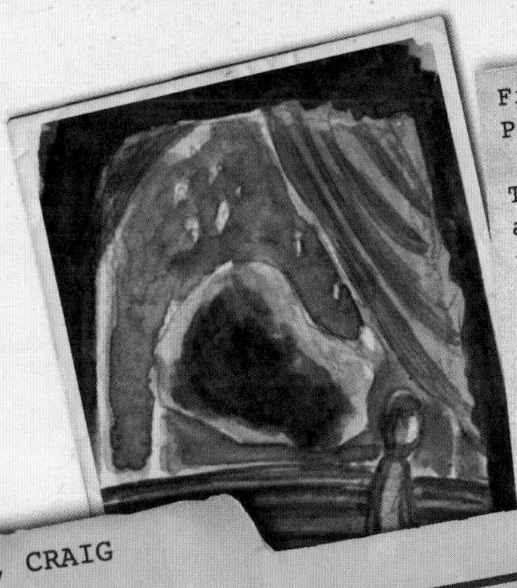

File #1968.1.19
Pressgang, Craig

The leaked photo of Pressgang's
appendix has been recovered and
remains unreleased. Negatives ha
also been recovered and destroy

Security for the wedding ceremo
is being handled by the Secret
and advance recon units have
cleared several locations in
New York City.

SSGANG, CRAIG

CLASSIFIED

Of course the wedding was big.
National headlines.

We invited only closest friends.

Some family.

And Craig's mom.

I think we should have gone to Sanibel Island instead.

No...

I'll be too big to come here next year.

Soon after graduating from college, Craig married the love of his life and college sweetheart, Jo. They went on to become the darlings of America! The dream couple in a dream home, living the American dream!

Craig was intent on showing the world that being large wasn't a handicap, but an advantage. And that if you work hard enough and long enough, eventually anything is possible!

Little did anyone know how successful Craig would become. And famous! His famous Tour of the World was about to begin! Soon the name Craig Pressgang would be known in every household!

I wish we were alone more.
FREAK SHOW

Since 1916

Thank you.

Thank YOU.

The Haggar custom suits didn't fit him by the time we got back, two weeks later.

Everything began to fall apart.

I've got something to tell you.

I'm a spy.

For real?

Yeah.

As he talked, I was so relieved that he had a secret. That he didn't tell me everything either.

And when he was done, I told him.
Well, I'm pregnant.

For real?

Maybe because he hadn't realized it yet...
It didn't feel like everything was falling apart.

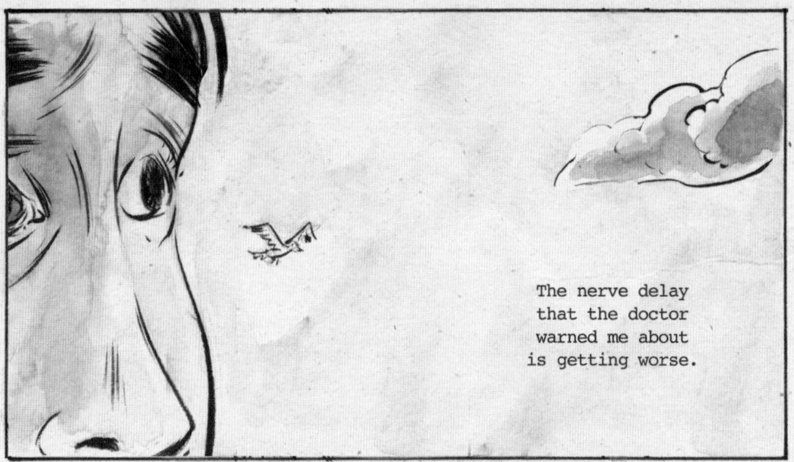
The nerve delay
that the doctor
warned me about
is getting worse.

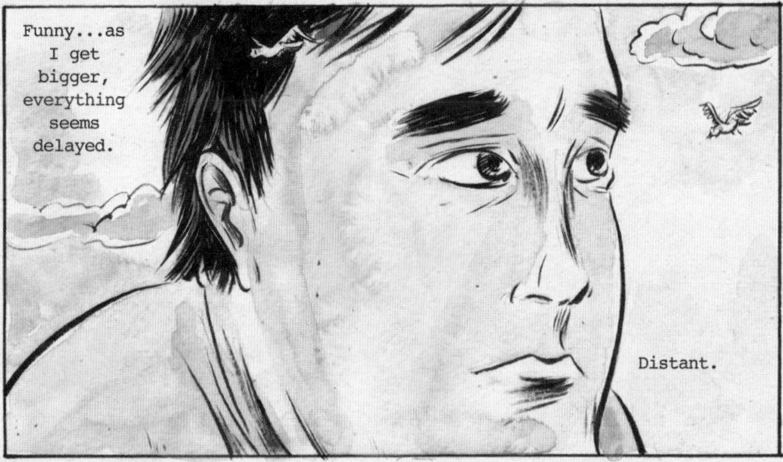
Funny...as
I get
bigger,
everything
seems
delayed.
Distant.

I'm everywhere now.
A celebrity.
More people know me
now than any other
single person on the
planet.

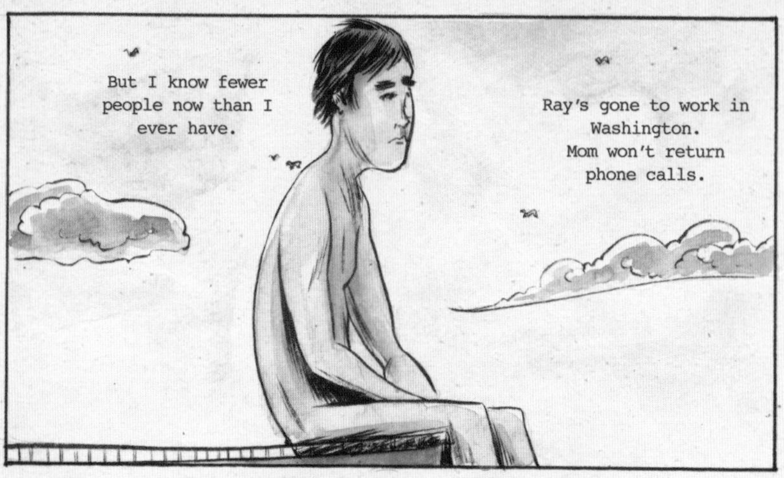
But I know fewer people now than I ever have.
Ray's gone to work in Washington. Mom won't return phone calls.

I end up holding onto Jo. But even that thread is starting to disappear.

I don't have an eye for detail now. Everything's fuzzy.

Everything that everyone else holds onto, I can't even see.
Voices are starting to sound small, too.

Like mice.
And I'm worried...

I worry that it's spreading.

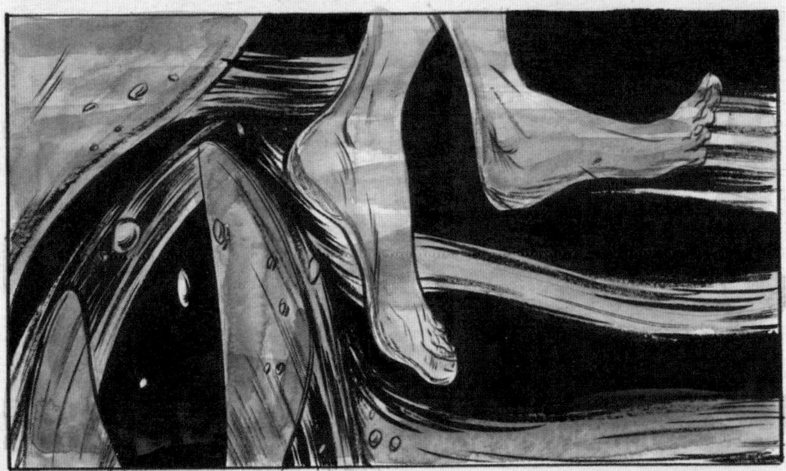

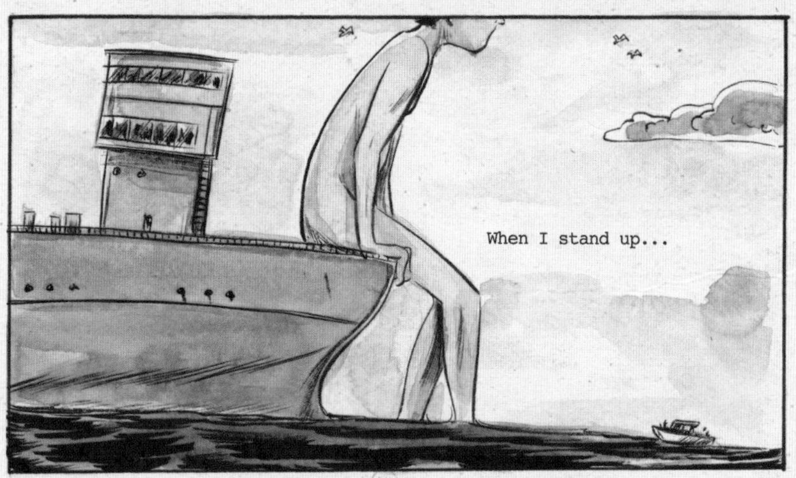
When I stand up...

It's a beautiful
and lonely
perspective...

I feel like I'm
staying the same...

And everyone else is getting smaller.

Leaving me.

Disappearing.

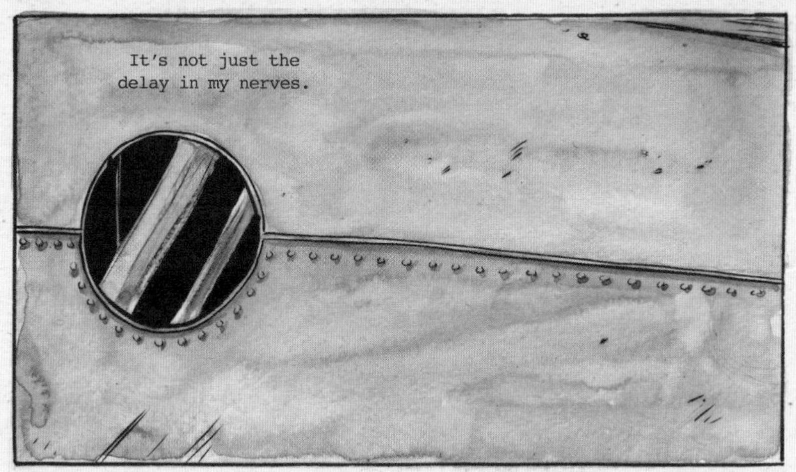
It's not just the
delay in my nerves.

I look at
her...

I look at
Jo...

And my head is waiting...
Craig Pressgang Journal 1/6/64 – 2/6/65
Waiting for my heart to say something...

To send it some kind of signal.

I worry that one day I'll be waiting to feel something, and there will be nothing.

GIANT
MAN

The scaffolding will allow you to stand at full height, for maximum visibility.

Onlookers (and our agent) will ascend the stairs to ask questions directly into your ear.

Our agent will take her turn...

And deposit a small canister in your inner ear.

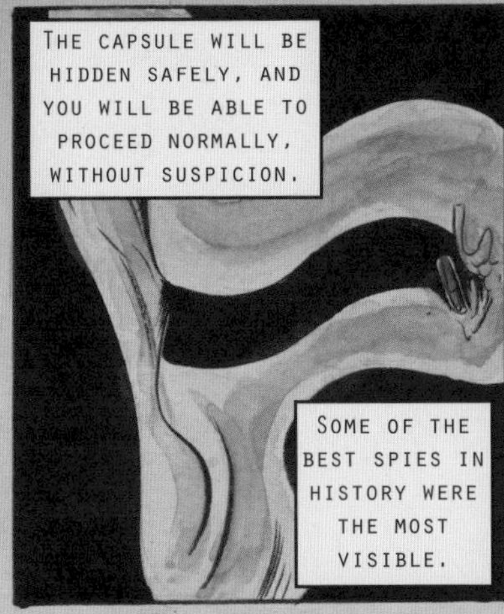
The capsule will be hidden safely, and you will be able to proceed normally, without suspicion.
Some of the best spies in history were the most visible.

Houdini.

Josephine Baker.

Billie Holiday.

You are officially our most visible agent.

Everything we did was strange.

But the overseas tour was the most surreal.

It seemed like I was getting a little taste of what he must have felt constantly.

The questions they asked were the worst.

How do you go to the bath- room?
And where?

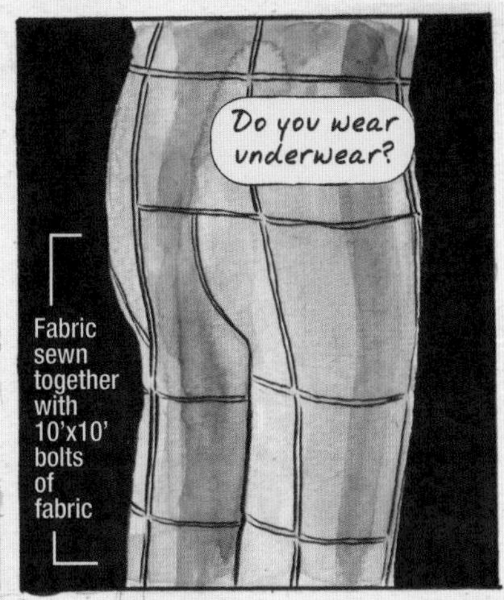
Do you wear underwear?
Fabric sewn together with 10'x10' bolts of fabric

How do you get a haircut?

What about sex?

Well, I'm looking for a three-story woman...
ha ha ha ha ha ha ha ha ha ha ha ha ha ha ha ha ha ha ha
ha ha ha ha ha ha ha ha ha
ha ha ha ha ha ha ha ha ha ha ha ha

Giant Man in Thanksgiving Parade

Then the parade happened. I remember having watched it as a kid on our fuzzy black-and-white television, and now here we were.
My husband was walking between Snoopy and Underdog.

Looking up at him...

I knew it was all coming down...

POP
Before it even happened.
But what could I do?

This wasn't my life.

Not the one I'd imagined.

Not the one I wanted.

That was the day I knew he'd left me.

He'd already walked out.

And I was alone.

Disaster!

When we got home, it reminded me of when I was little.

TINK
TINK

After playing outside all day.
Coming in for dinner, I would go into my room to change clothes, and I could barely see.
TINK
TINK

GIANT MAN FALLS IN PARADE

The annual Thanksgiving Day parade was marred by near-tragedy yesterday as Craig Pressgang, the star attraction of the parade, stumbled and fell. The exact cause of Pressgang's accident is unknown, but the giant man's handlers are expected to give a press conference by the end of the week with their findings.

Miraculously, no one was hurt in the fall that severely damaged several buildings and crushed

*

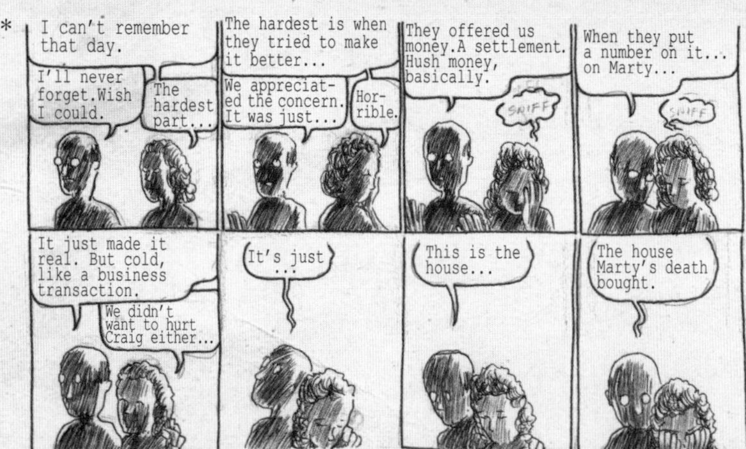

And everything inside seemed darker.
No matter how wide I opened my eyes...
I couldn't see inside.

Maybe I used it as an excuse.

To put more distance between us.

To protect myself.

I hated the house.

I started to change it.

And stopped worrying...

...about the
size of the
door frames.

That's when I built the house inside the house. To protect myself.

I couldn't tell if he was looking into me or right past us.

But it started to make me feel like a child again. Small.
Like God was looking down -- seeing everything I did.

The CIA is letting me go.
What are we going to do?

It wasn't my fault. I don't know what happened. I heard a pop. And then...
I know. You didn't mean...

I need you to tell me that, though. Before anything else.
I know. It wasn't your fault, Craig. It wasn't.

But it was me. If I hadn't been there...
You have to put it into perspec-tive. There was nothing you could have done.

I don't even remember. I woke up on the truck.
The government took care of everything.

Yeah...

I don't believe the agency.
What?

The child? They said he survived.

He did. The paper said...
There was blood on my clothes. I saw...

He's okay. They couldn't cover that up.

Well, I'm unemployed. Who's going to use me for endorsements?
But what now? What do we do?
I wouldn't even want to anymore.

dada!

I'm just -- it'll be nice to have you home.
dada!

We worried about Iris.

But the doctors couldn't find anything abnormal.
They knew what to look for this time.

I still worried about her.

I knew this was the end, really. Like the last fifteen minutes of a familiar movie. You know it's going to end badly.
But you sit through the credits anyway, hoping that the ending will have been changed.

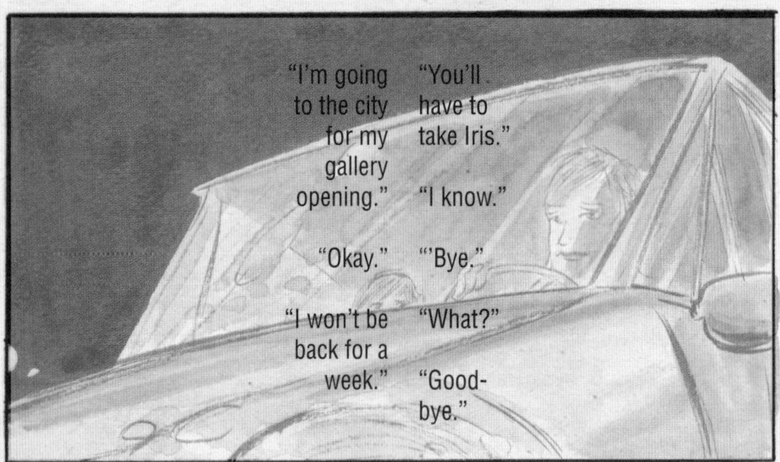
"I'm going to the city for my gallery opening."
"You'll have to take Iris."
"I know."
"Okay."
"'Bye."
"I won't be back for a week."
"What?"
"Good-bye."

Jo Pressgang

One of Pressgang's earliest pieces recalls her first meeting with her husband in a suburban pizza parlor. The straightforward nature of the construction and strict representational qualities of this piece only echo her later playfulness with form and media.

This large piece details Pressgang's early childhood on the farm. This is a piece from her middle period, and shows her progression to later works. The idealized setting and the exaggerated scale of the tree all represent her early attempts at playing with scale and perspective.

This piece represents the beginning of her modern phase. The structures are starting to show wear and distress. Naturalistic proportions have returned, but organic growth has started to appear in unlikely places. Jo, what's going on with your art?

I was looking at your work the other day. I don't understand it. Maybe, well.... Maybe it's just hard for me to see under my magnifying glasses. But why is everything falling apart? I don't get it.

No. I just... I'm trying something new. I was getting tired of just doing the same stuff over and over again. I'm trying to...I don't know. I'm trying to reflect some of myself. Or put some of myself into it.

I don't like them. If you want to talk to me, talk to me. You don't have to be clever about it. If you're so miserable, then what are you doing here?

Gallery Exhibit
March 6 – May 19

He literally
grew away
from us.

His vocal chords were so big. His lungs. Everything.
He had to whisper so we could understand him and not burst our eardrums.
5

I had to shout at him. All he could hear was buzzing.

Small Art Makes Big Splash

The prestigious Vowels Gallery in Chicago recently showcased the new, unique talent of Jo Pressgang, the wife of the famous "Giant Man," Craig Pressgang. At first sight, Jo's work is very reminiscent of the renowned Thorne Miniatures, some of which are housed at the nearby Chicago Art Institute.

However, upon closer inspection it is evident that Pressgang's work is aiming even higher. These are not simple historical re-creations on a miniature scale. Each of Pressgang's small constructions houses an enormous depth of emotion and feeling. This is especially evident when viewing her work not only in the context of her later, more famous "destruction pieces," but within the context of her life as the wife of one of the most famous men in the country. How does this inform her work? And how did this demure artist finally step out of the shadow of one of the most famous personalities in the last dec

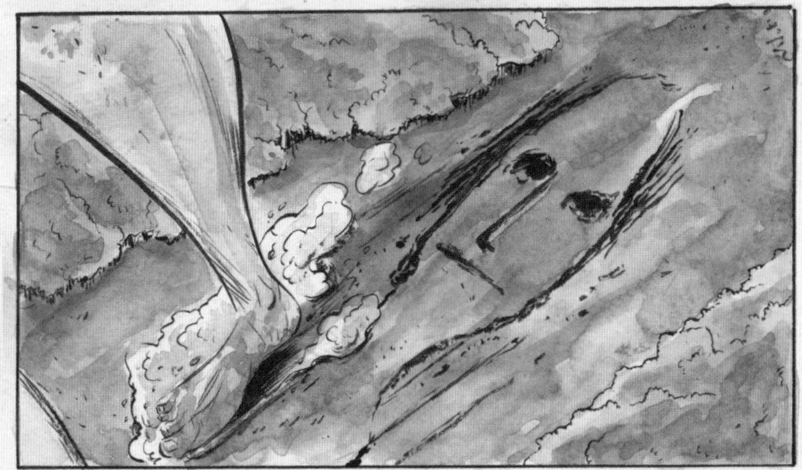

I MISS YOU!
?
GOING FOR WALK

FORD

YOU
NEED
TO

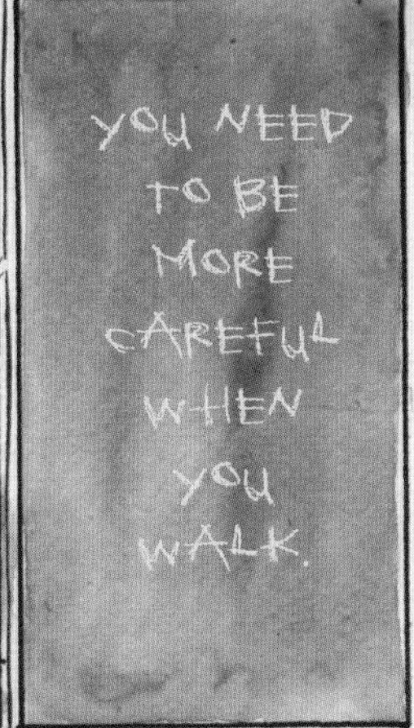
YOU NEED
TO BE
MORE
CAREFUL
WHEN
YOU
WALK.

I
KNOW

JO–
JO–
I'M
DYING

I DON'T
WANT
TO HURT
ANYONE
ELSE

I'M
SCARED
I'LL
HURT
YOU OR

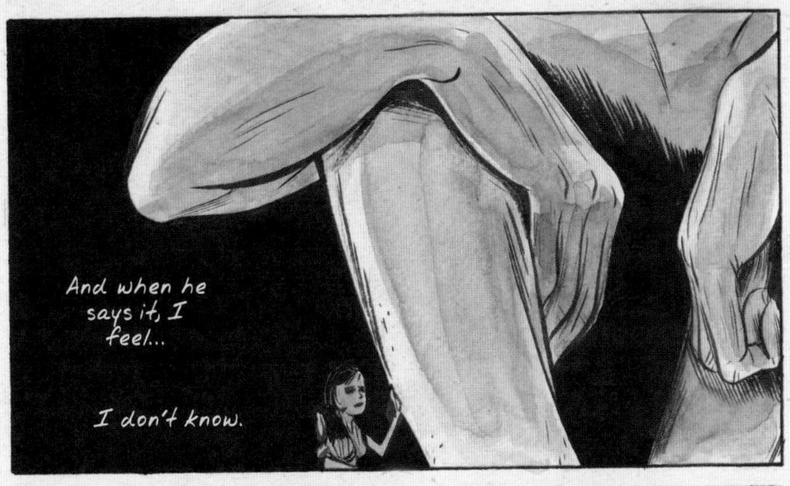
And when he says it, I feel...
I don't know.

A wave of sadness.
And relief.
And total guilt for feeling even a hint of that.

I loved Craig. But he wasn't there anymore.
He was a giant ghost.

I told him I understood. Who knows?
Iris was old enough to understand, I think.

She related to her father like you would to a mountain. Or a familiar playground.

She'd miss him, but like you'd miss the house you grew up in as a kid.

I think.

I hope.

At the end I couldn't write big enough for him to focus on. He was leaving, but it was just a formality now.

WE COULDN'T EVEN TALK AT THE END.
IT WAS STRANGELY SILENT.

When I kissed him goodbye...

...I know he
didn't feel it.

And then he was gone.

I saw him pause, and
I hoped it was because he'd seen it...

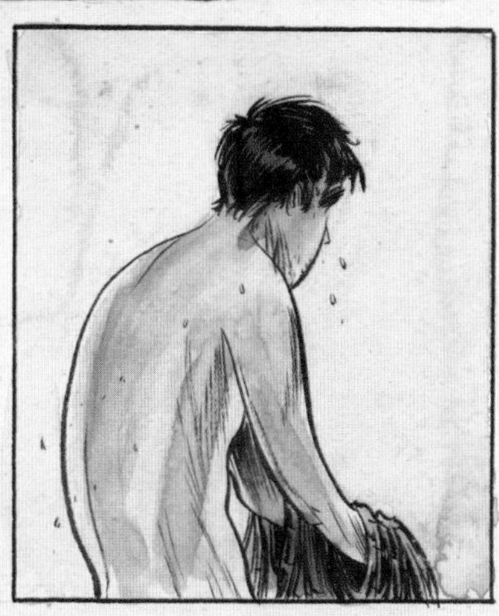

I imagined
where he went...

And what he was doing...

And I know he still felt.
I know sensation was there.

He was just farther away...

...and it took a little longer.

I hoped it was enough.

3RD STORY

It took me a helluva lot longer to find my father than I thought it would...
Considering his size.

It's like losing a three-story building.

But if that building collapsed in the woods, who would see it? How would you find it?
I guess that was what he wanted.

I followed eye-witness accounts west from Chicago.

Like following a decades-old storm.

The trail just ends up being stories.

I began to understand why they name hurricanes.

Thanks for seeing me.
It makes something incomprehensible a little more manageable.
Glad to have ya.

Well, it was years ago...

He was crazy.
Out of his mind.
No offense.

Next stop...

Las Vegas.

What the hell was I looking for?

Memories clearer than my own, I guess.

And the site of the famous Vegas photo.
GATLIN JR.
Riviera
24 HOUR
DANDYFIES

I was ten when this was taken.

WANTED:
INFORMATION regarding Craig Pressgang, the "Giant Man." Please call 314-555-1416 with any stories or anecdotes, firsthand or otherwise. A generous fee will be paid for any information that is used for publication in a

We'd been drinking...
CLICK
"A lot.
GIRL
XXX
RLS
XXX
"I don't even remember taking the photo.

"We followed him out of town.

"We were scared, but drunk enough not to care.

"We thought he was screaming at us.
"I don't know.

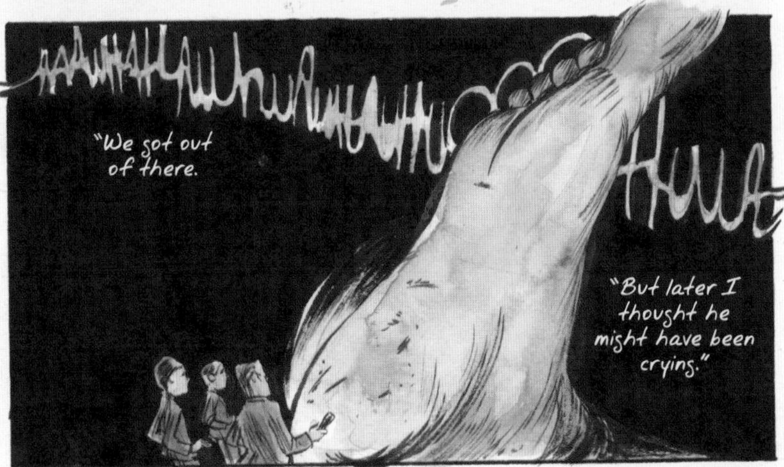
"We got out of there.
"But later I thought he might have been crying."

I found bits of him all over the desert.

But no body.

CLICK
HA
HA
SPLASH
HA
HA

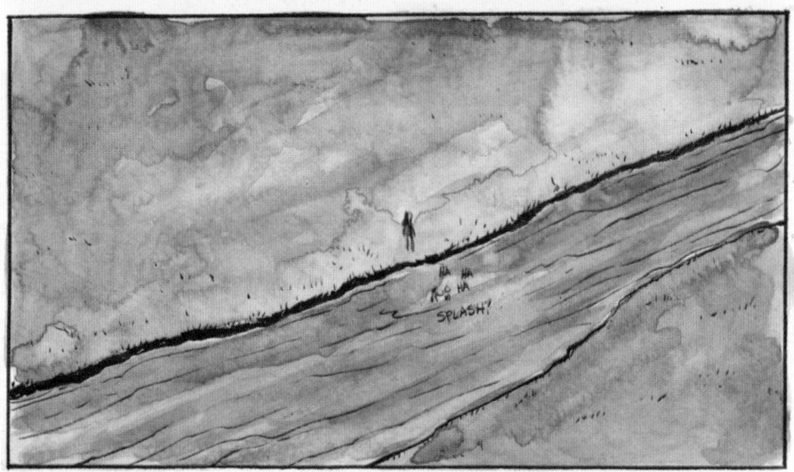
HA HA
HA
SPLASH

HA HA HA
HA

Then I got a phone call from a guy I'd talked to earlier.

A crackpot.
Iris? I talked to you a few weeks ago?

I worked with your father.

I was CIA. I helped him. I know you're writing a book, so I hesitated to tell you.

But you should know. You deserve to know.

I'm assuming you've read this?
iant Man
Pillar of America

Giant Man

Pillar of America

The Official
Souvenir Biography
of the World's
Tallest Man

Cripes! This sun is killing me!
Did you get the shot?
Got it.

The book was a total puff piece. A manufactured history we made.
Who's "we"?
The Agency.

We left all the middle bits out, of course.
Your mother tell you he was a spy?

Yes. I half believed her.

Well, you can believe her.
Follow me.

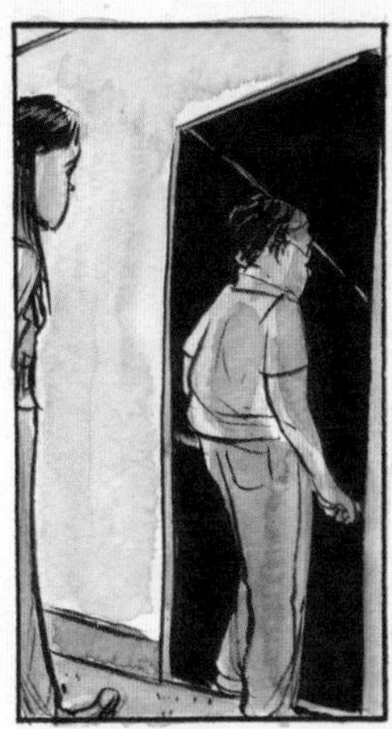

Best hiding place...

CLICK

Out in the open.

This will locate your father. I assume you're still looking?
We installed tracking devices in him.

"He had no idea.

"We didn't want to lose him.

"In case of accidents.

"We'd talked about using him in Vietnam.
"But his extremities were too vulnerable to infection.

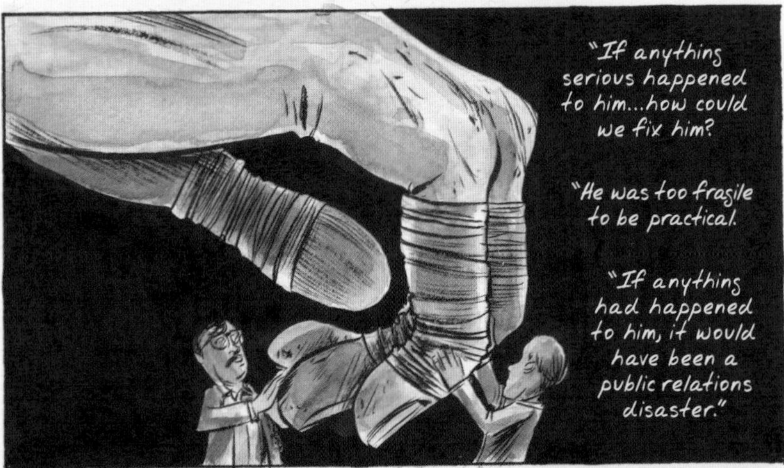
"If anything serious happened to him...how could we fix him?
"He was too fragile to be practical.
"If anything had happened to him, it would have been a public relations disaster."

He was a glorified courier, really.

But after that summer in Russia, it was all over.

"Our agent in Russia...

"Was compromised, apparently.

"I won't bore you with the details.

"But Craig's cover was blown before we could get him out.

PFFT

"There was no international incident.
"So we considered ourselves lucky.

"But then the Thanksgiving Day Parade happened.

"A time-delay explosive must have been hidden in his ear.

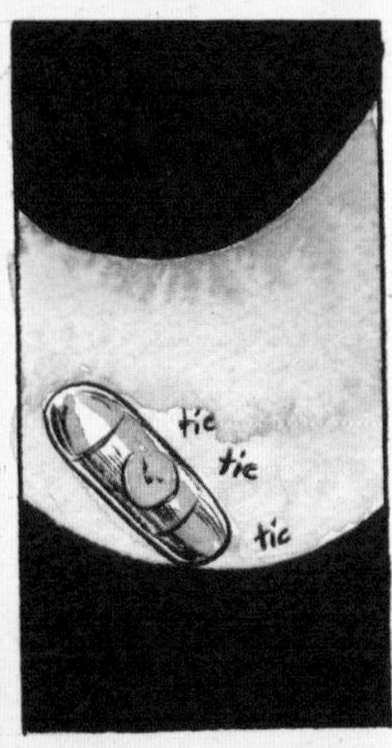
tic
tic
tic

"We were going to decommission him anyway, but the fall made it easy, I guess.
POOM

"We looked after him when we could, after that.
NEWS 2

AD
UCTION
ETOUR
"And cleaned up after him.

"If he wanted solitude...

"...We'd help him maintain it.

"It was safer for everyone that way."

HONEY COMB

The publisher funded the last leg of my journey.
"The book is nearly done," I'd tell them.

"You've got to find him," they'd reply.
I now had a way to track him, but I didn't want to use it right away.

Instead, I logged all confirmed sightings before he disappeared off the radar.

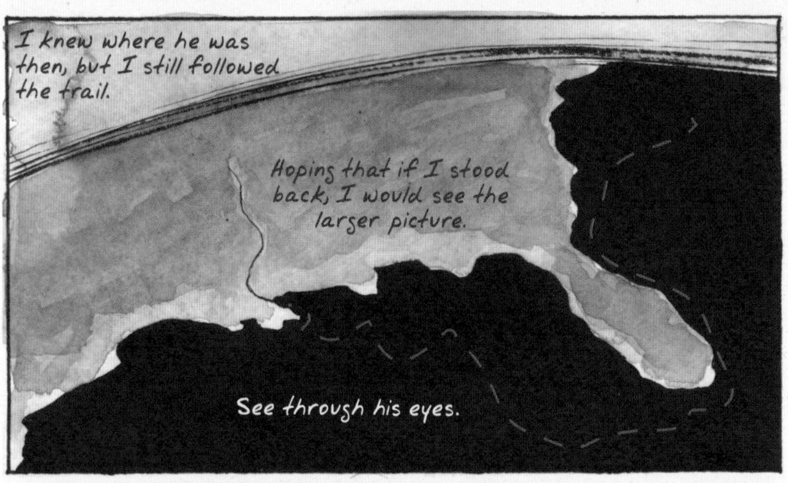
I knew where he was then, but I still followed the trail.
Hoping that if I stood back, I would see the larger picture.
See through his eyes.

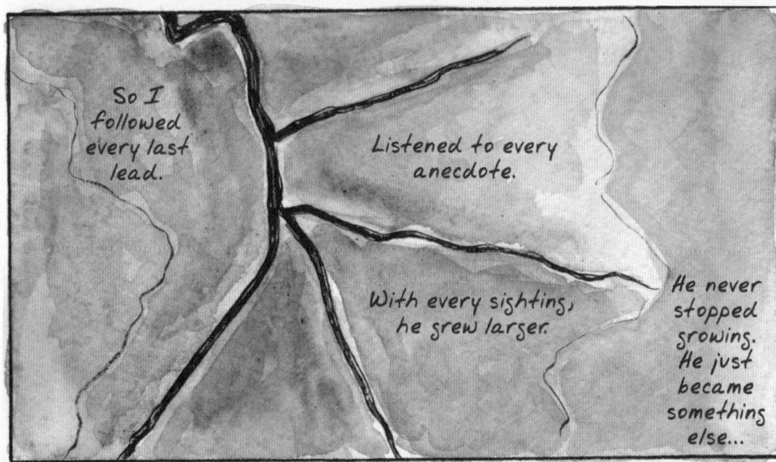
So I followed every last lead.
Listened to every anecdote.
With every sighting, he grew larger.
He never stopped growing. He just became something else...

More unreal.

I felt like I was pursuing fiction.

The map gave me an easy perspective.
Easier than his wounded and bloody feet must have been.

Easier than scratched and unfeeling fingertips.

He left more enigmatic clues.

Wads of swatted
birds, like insects.

Mysterious holes in
the ground.

And in the end...

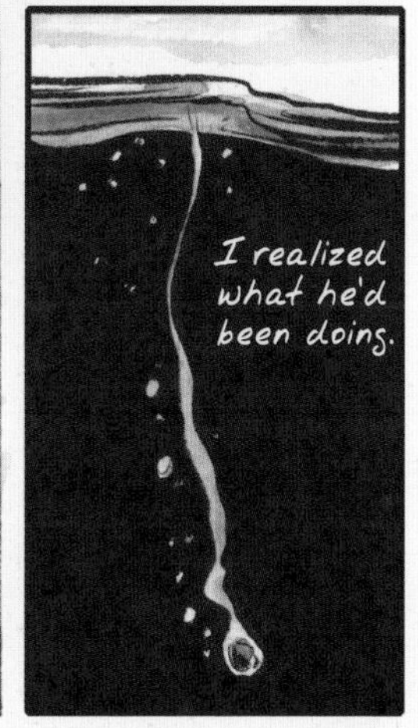
I realized what he'd been doing.

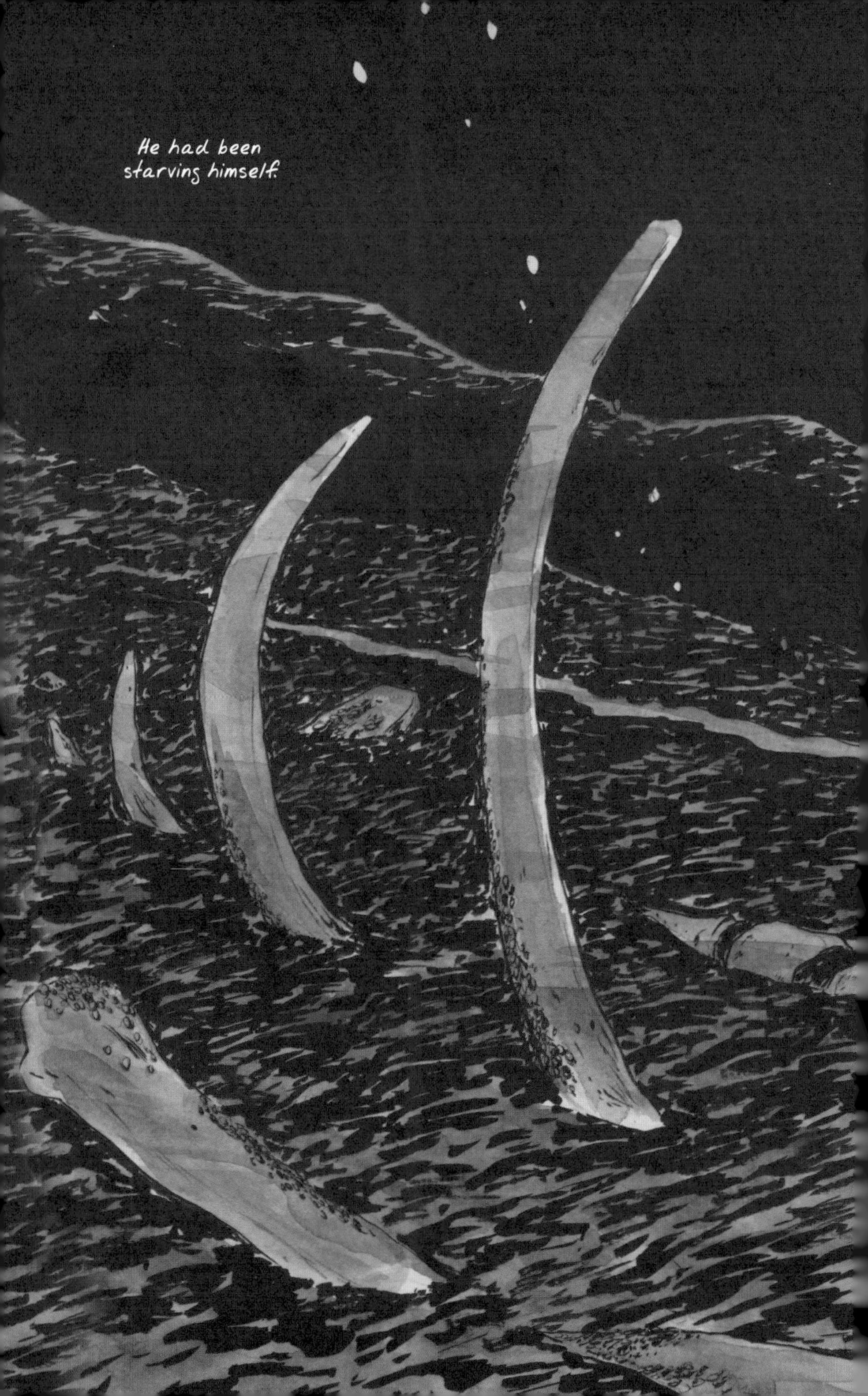
He had been
starving himself.

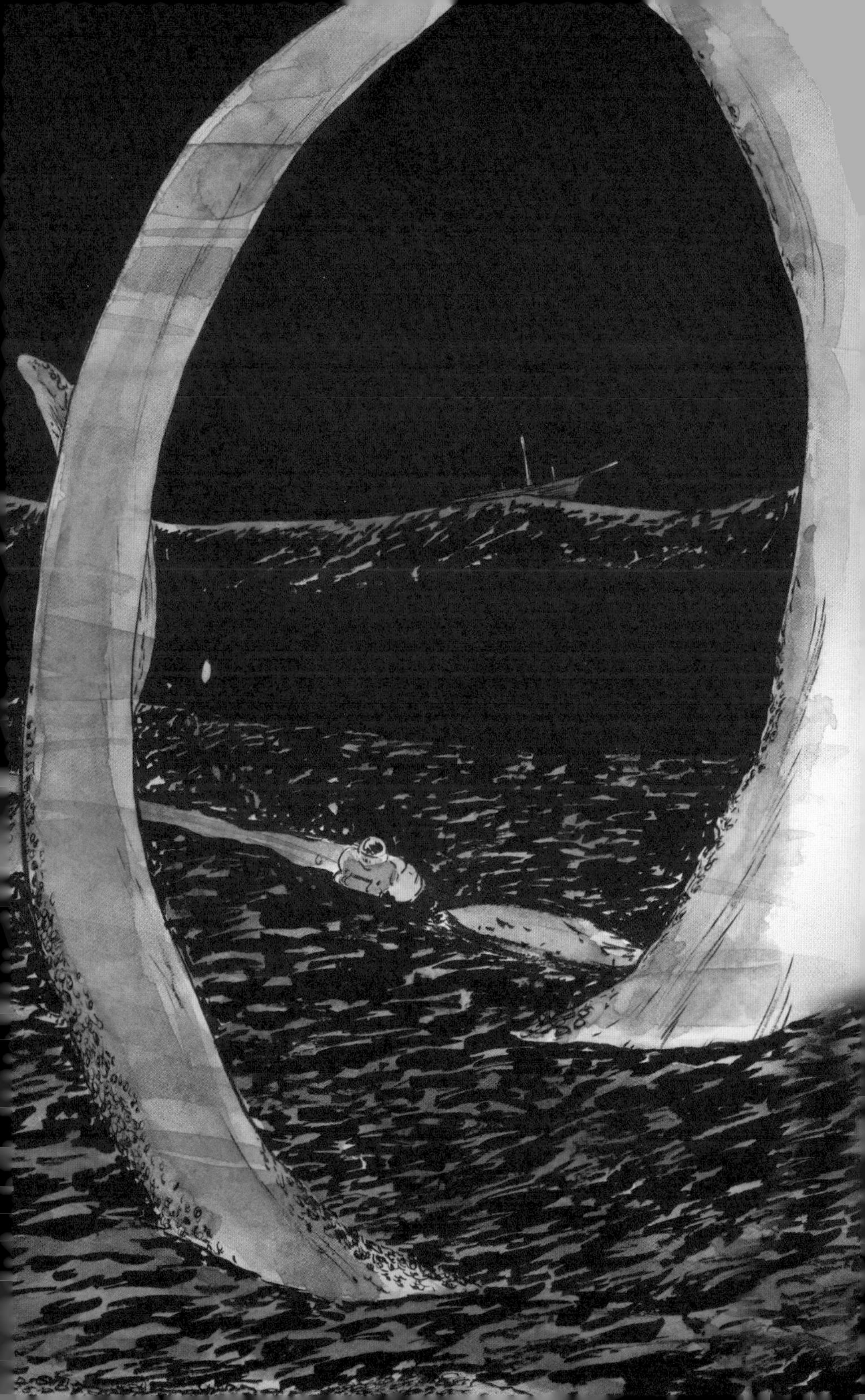

I followed my father's trail around the globe.
And traced his confusion in the scarred mountainsides and trampled earth.

And at the end, I think he panicked.
As if he had finally remembered who he was and what he needed to do.
He was operating at the most basic level.

He knew where he was going.
He wasn't going to die on a deserted island.
He was heading up the river.

Taking himself north.
To the Great Lakes.

Back to Jo.

Back to
his family.

And
grandkids
...

Taking himself north. To the Grea Lakes. Back to Jo. Back to his family.

And grandkids, too small to see.

The closer I looked at everything...

The less I seemed to understand.

I guess ultimately the only clue to his identity...

Was what he
left behind.

3 STORY
Matt Kindt
Secret Files of the Giant Man

MATT KINDT

THE SECRET FILES OF

THE GIANT MAN IN PARIS

They called us in because he was having stomach pains.

It was the first time I'd seen him. I couldn't believe it.
His handlers were very secretive.
And protective.

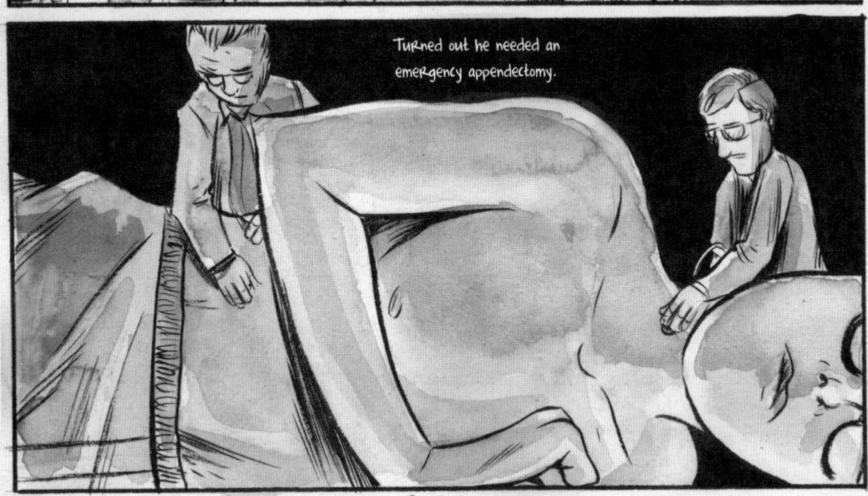
Turned out he needed an emergency appendectomy.

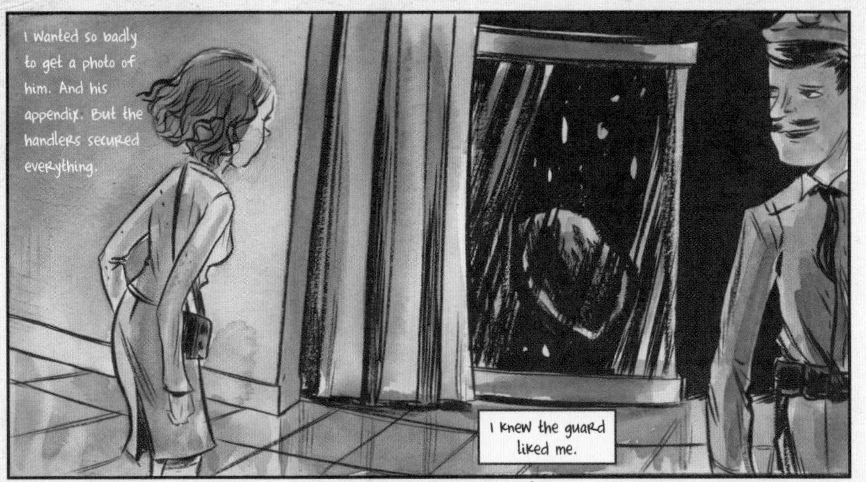
I wanted so badly to get a photo of him. And his appendix. But the handlers secured everything.
I knew the guard liked me.

And I got my photo.
CLICK

But I couldn't stop thinking about the giant man himself.

I wondered if he would hear me...

And then I wondered...

if he would see me...

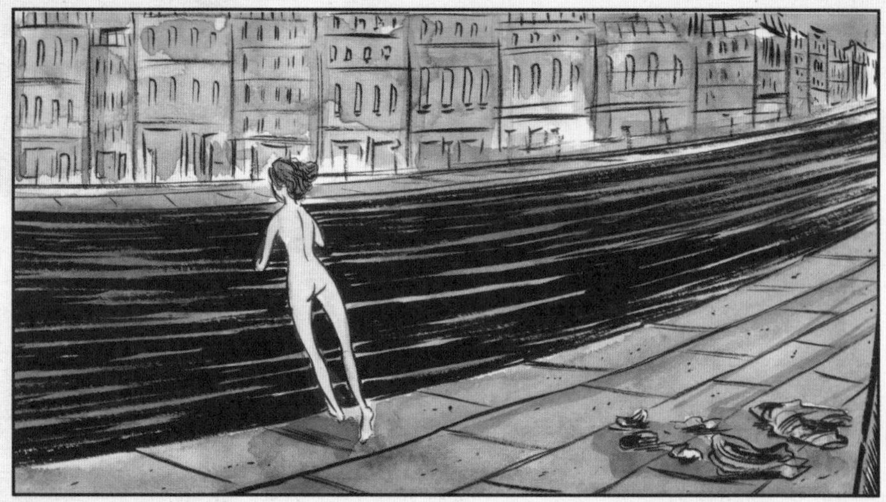

The next day his
manager hired me to be
his personal assistant
for the remainder of
his stay in Paris.

I couldn't believe it.

I was never able
to look at the
Louvre the same
way again.

It's bigger
than I thought it
would be.

And then he had to leave.
It kind of reminded me of when I was a little girl.

I used to make friends out of anything.

A rock. A coffee bean. Anything.

I remember the window in my room when I was a kid. It never stayed up on its own.
So my parents grabbed a random scrap of wood to prop it up for me in the summers.

Needless to say, that little scrap of wood became my friend.

The guardian of my room.

So, that Fall after Craig Pressgang left...

I watched him walk off.
Back to his ship.
And I wondered how I looked to him.

His guide?
His friend?
Or just a Random scrap.

MATT KINDT

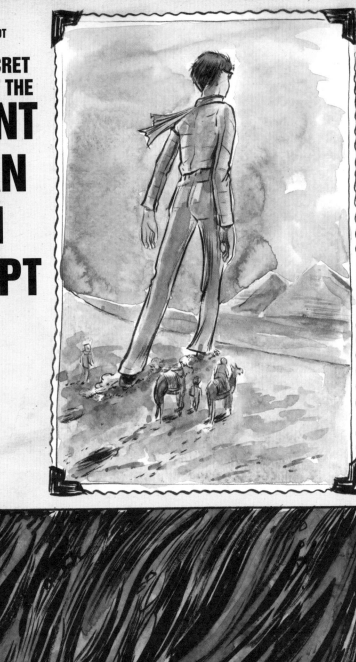

THE SECRET FILES OF THE GIANT MAN IN EGYPT

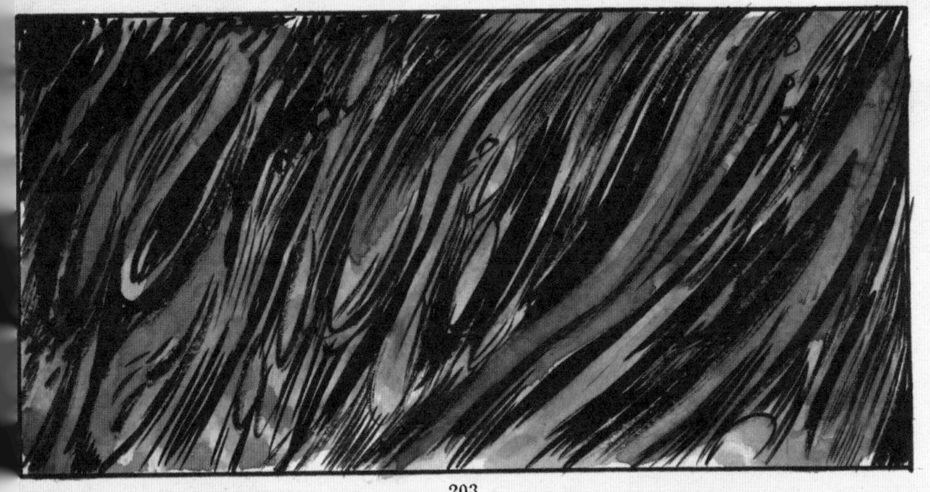

Have you seen him yet?
No. Are you kidding?

When do I have time for vacation?

My wife thinks he's a spy.
Your wife thinks he's handsome.

Better him than Kennedy.

I don't know. How you going to live up to someone so big?

Too big to be a threat, I say.

Usi!
Usi!

Yes, sir.
He needs another full meal. More fruit this time.

More fruit, like I told you last time! Hurry!
Yes, sir.

You'd think after all these years...

...we'd stop doing this kind of thing.

Kind of funny...

CAIRO HOTEL
Like one tourist attraction visiting another.

RO HOTEL

TEL

You okay?
OTEL

We have the parade later today...
Ugh...

Kind of feel sick again.
Call back the doctors.
And get another bin.

ugghh...

Get the truck back here!

We don't get paid enough for this.

MATT KINDT'S

GIANT MAN IN THE PHILIPPINES

In 1965, President Johnson was planning the escalation of action in Vietnam. Among the numerous ideas planned to get the general public and world opinion on our side was enlisting Craig's help in the effort. If Craig failed, it would be a PR disaster.

I was at the Department of Defense at the time.
I was to keep it completely secret until success was had.

Thanks so much. Your presence in Vietnam will make all the difference.
No problem. Let's take care of it.

Secret even from Craig's CIA handler in the States.

Thanks so much. His visit to the Philippines will mean everything to those kids.

No problem. Take care of him.

But how do you smuggle a three-story-tall celebrity into a conflict in Vietnam?

A skeleton crew of trusted sailors.
10,000 yards of tarp.

An industrial-sized straw.
And a thousand pounds of vegetable purée.

God knows how many millions went into the special leg braces designed to keep him stable and protected.

Those damn leg braces lasted five minutes and ended up giving him one of the worst cuts he'd ever receive.

The medical supplies and bandages from that injury alone would drain the military's resources for the entire month.
But my orders were to continue.

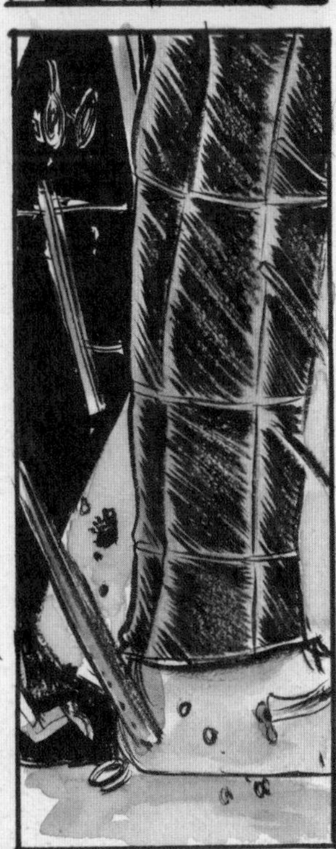

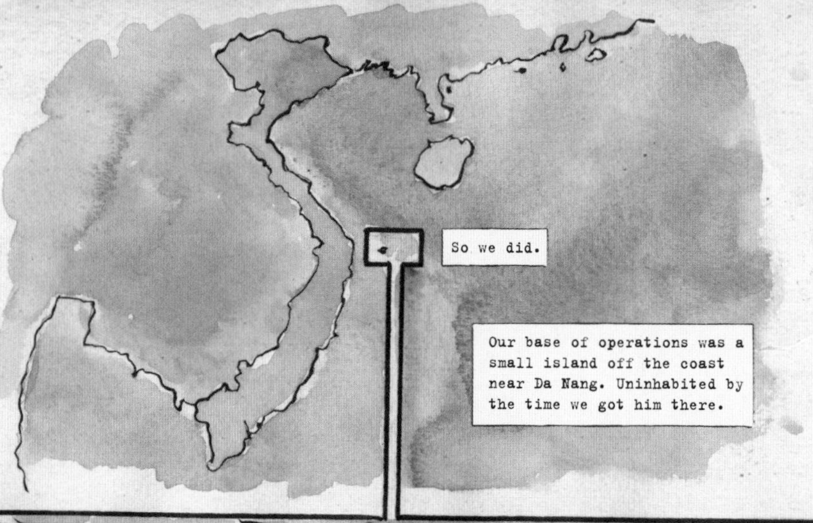

So we did.

Our base of operations was a small island off the coast near Da Nang. Uninhabited by the time we got him there.

We used an incredible amount of smoke to shield Craig from the mainland.

Our own Skull Island.

CRASHHHH

The trip to
the Philippines
was just a
cover story.

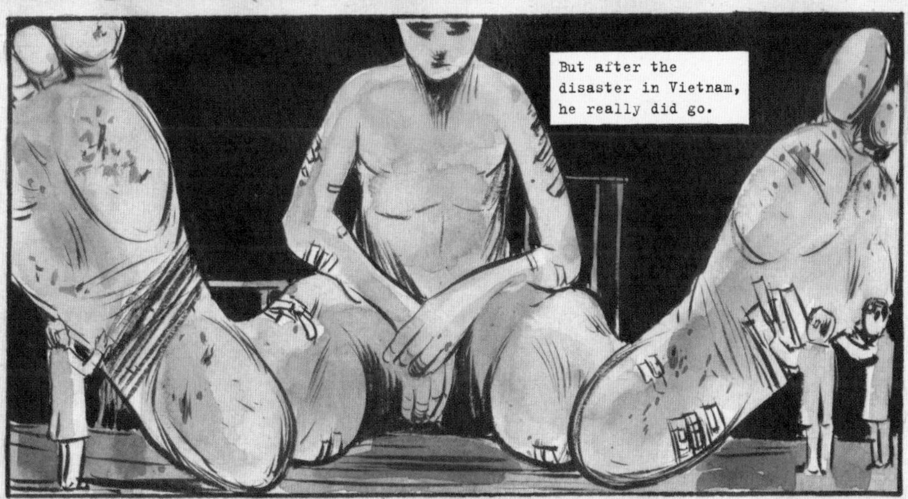
But after the
disaster in Vietnam,
he really did go.

He spent a month
there recovering.

Later I heard they had a photographer covering Craig in Vietnam.

Photos never surfaced, but I can only imagine what impact those images would have had...

His failure might have turned the public against the war and ended it all years earlier.

It could have been his greatest achievement.

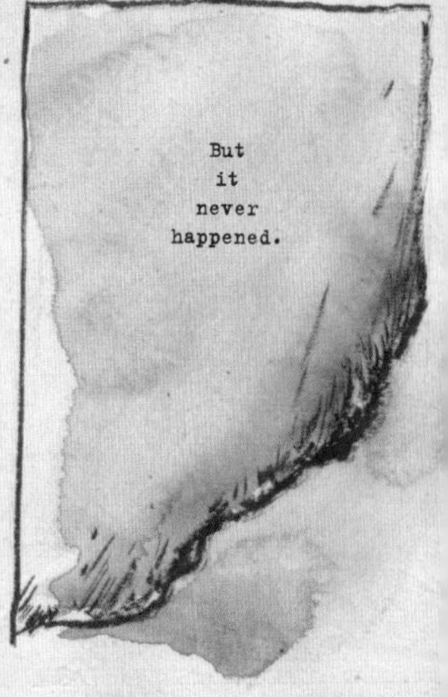
But it never happened.

3 STORY™ SKETCHBOOK

Notes by Matt Kindt

These were the original character sketches I did when I was outlining the book. It was important to get the scale of Craig figured out as he ages through the story. This was the guide I used. I was also playing with his outfits and glasses—trying to figure out not only what a giant man wears but how his clothes would be manufactured. I imagined a series of thin panels made of parachute material.

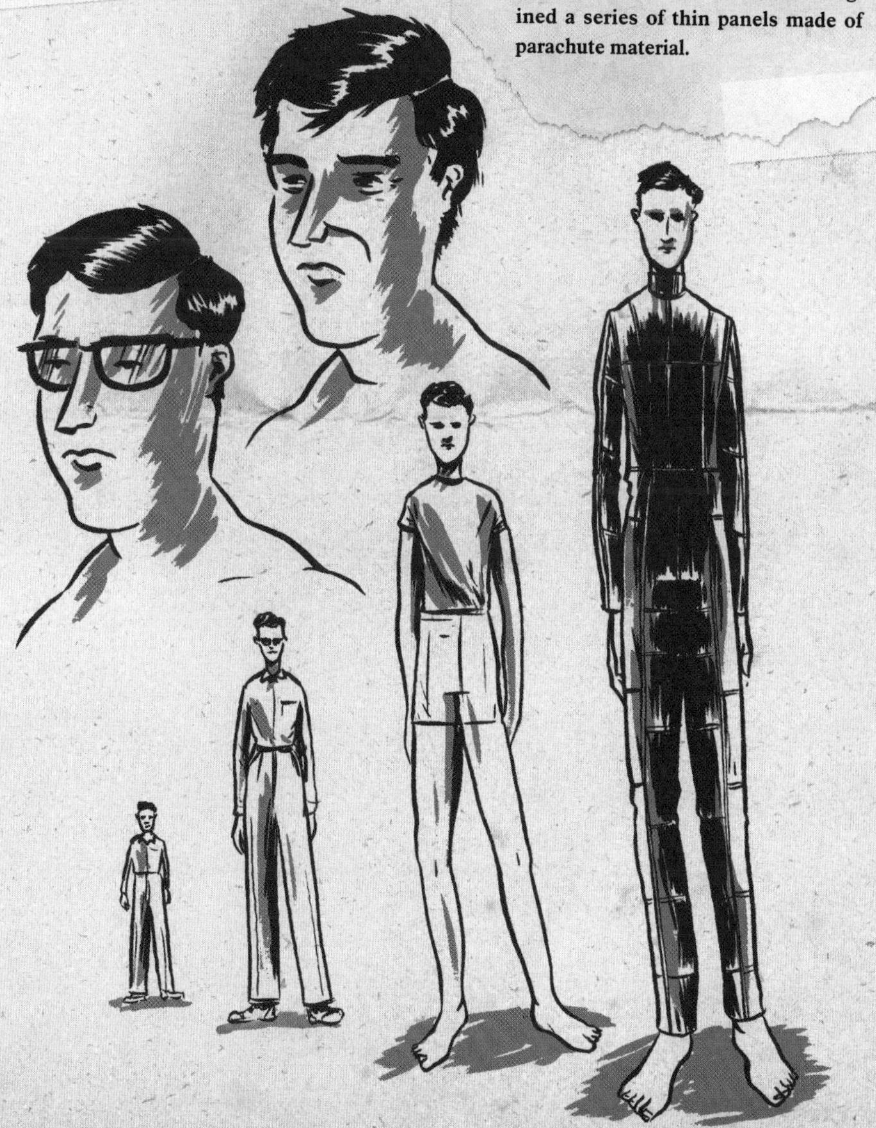

Scale was one of the most important things I had to consider visually. His scale would dictate his interactions with his mother and his wife. These interactions needed to convey both the story and the emotional space between the characters.

These were the original test pages I did as a "proof of concept" when I pitched the idea of the book to Dark Horse. Both of these scenes appear in the book with slight variations. One of the first visuals I imagined was an immense set of bones deep under the ocean or in the desert. In the first draft, Craig's bones ended up in the desert with a theme park built around them. In the end I thought the ocean would be a more dignified place for him.

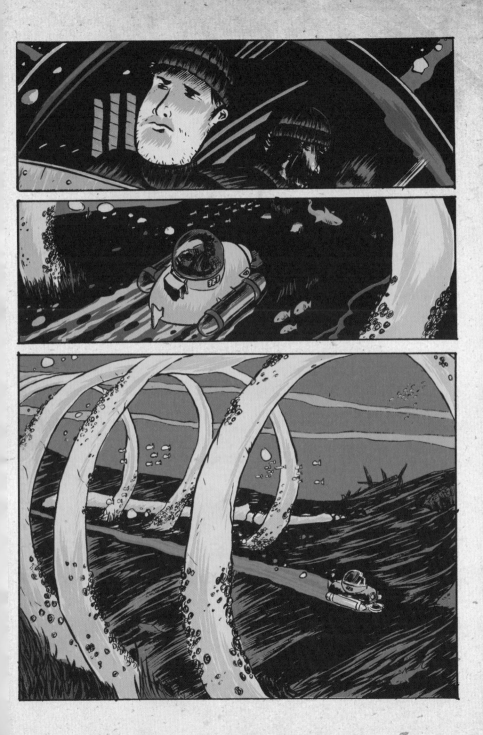

matt kindt

"I'll read anything Kindt does."—Douglas Wolk, author of *Reading Comics*

MIND MGMT
VOLUME 1: THE MANAGER
ISBN 978-1-59582-797-5
$19.99

VOLUME 2: THE FUTURIST
ISBN 978-1-61655-198-8
$19.99

VOLUME 3: THE HOME MAKER
ISBN 978-1-61655-390-6
$19.99

VOLUME 4: THE MAGICIAN
ISBN 978-1-61655-391-3
$19.99

VOLUME 5: THE ERASER
ISBN 978-1-61655-696-9
$19.99

VOLUME 6: THE IMMORTALS
ISBN 978-1-61655-798-0
$19.99

POPPY! AND THE LOST LAGOON
With Brian Hurtt
ISBN 978-1-61655-943-4
$14.99

PAST AWAYS
With Scott Kolins
ISBN 978-1-61655-792-8
$19.99

THE COMPLETE PISTOLWHIP
With Jason Hall
ISBN 978-1-61655-720-1
$27.99

3 STORY: THE SECRET HISTORY OF THE GIANT MAN NEW EXPANDED EDITION
ISBN 978-1-50670-622-1
$19.99

2 SISTERS
ISBN 978-1-61655-721-8
$27.99

DEPT. H
With Sharlene Kindt
VOLUME 1: PRESSURE
ISBN 978-1-61655-989-2
$19.99

VOLUME 2: AFTER THE FLOOD
ISBN 978-1-61655-990-8
$19.99

VOLUME 3: DECOMPRESSED
ISBN 978-1-61655-991-5
$19.99

VOLUME 4: LIFEBOAT
ISBN 978-1-61655-992-2
$19.99

ETHER
With David Rubín
VOLUME 1: DEATH OF THE LAST GOLDEN BLAZE
ISBN 978-1-50670-174-5
$14.99

AVAILABLE AT YOUR LOCAL COMICS SHOP OR BOOKSTORE!

To find a comics shop in your area, visit comicshoplocator.com. For more information or to order direct visit DarkHorse.com or call 1-800-862-0052 Mon.–Fri. 9 AM to 5 PM Pacific Time.

DARKHORSE.COM

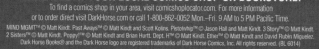